SPECTRUM
Test Practice

Grade 1

D1520262

Published by Spectrum
an imprint of
Frank Schaffer Publications®

SPECTRUM

Editors: Mary Rose Hassinger and Angella Phebus

Frank Schaffer Publications®

Spectrum is an imprint of Frank Schaffer Publications.

Send all inquiries to:
Frank Schaffer Publications
3195 Wilson Drive NW
Grand Rapids, Michigan 49534

Spectrum Test Practice—grade 1

ISBN: 1-57768-721-3

4 5 6 7 8 9 10 PAT 09 08 07 06 05

SPECTRUM TEST PRACTICE

Table of Contents
Grade 1

With increased accountability in ensuring academic success for all learners, testing now takes a significant amount of time for students in all settings. Standardized tests are designed to measure what students know. These tests are nationally normed. State tests are usually tied to specific academic standards identified for mastery.

For many students, testing can be a mystery. They fear not doing well and not knowing what to expect on the test. This *Spectrum Test Practice* book was developed to introduce students to both the format and the content they will encounter on tests. It was developed on the assumption that students have received prior instruction on the skills included. This book is designed to cover the content on a representative sample of state standards. The sampling of standards is found on pages 8–10 with a correlation to the skills covered in this book and a correlation to sample standardized tests. Spaces are provided to record the correlation to the tests being administered by the user of this book. Spaces are also provided to add standards that are specific to the user.

Features of *Spectrum Test Practice*

- Skill lessons, sample tests for subtopics, and comprehensive content area tests
- Clues for being successful with specific skills
- Correlation of skills to state standards and standardized tests
- Format and structure similar to other formal tests
- Written response required in the Science and Social Studies sections (except in Grade 1)
- Reproducible for use by a teacher for a classroom

Overview

This book is developed within content areas (Reading, Language, Math, Science, and Social Studies). A comprehensive practice test follows at the end of the content area, with an answer sheet for students to record responses. Within each content area, specific subtopics have been identified. Sample tests are provided for each subtopic. Within each subtopic, specific skill lessons are presented. These specific skill lessons include an example and a clue for being successful with the skill.

Comprehensive Practice Test

A comprehensive practice test is provided for each content area. The subtopics for each area are identified below:

- **Reading**
  - Word Analysis (letter recognition, letter sounds, rhyming words, and sight words)
  - Vocabulary (picture vocabulary, word reading, word meaning, synonyms, antonyms, and words in context)
  - Reading Comprehension (listening, picture, and sentence comprehension; fiction and nonfiction articles)

- **Language**
  - Listening Skills (auditory discrimination, comprehension)
  - Language Mechanics (capitalization and punctuation)
  - Language Expression (usage, sentences, and paragraphs)
  - Spelling (both correct and incorrect spelling)
  - Study Skills (book parts, reference materials, ABC order)

- **Math**
  - Concepts (numeration, number concepts, algebra, properties)
  - Computation (addition and subtraction of whole numbers)
  - Applications (geometry, measurement, and problem solving).
- **Science***
  - Environment
  - Seasons/Mammals
  - Matter: Liquids
- **Social Studies***
  - Family
  - Changes in the Community
  - Maps

*Since states and often districts determine units of study within Science and Social Studies, the content in this book may not be aligned with the content offered in all courses of study. The content within each area is grade level appropriate. It is based on a sampling of state standards.

Comprehensive Practice Test Includes

- Content Area (i.e. Language)
- Subtopics (i.e. Language Mechanics)
- Directions, examples, and test questions
- Separate answer sheet with "bubbles" to be filled in for answers

Sample Tests

Sample tests are included for all subtopics. These sample tests are designed to apply the knowledge and experience from the skill lessons in a more formal format. No clues are included. These sample tests are shorter than the comprehensive tests and longer than the skill lessons. The skills on the test items are presented in the same order as introduced in the book.

Sample Tests Include

- Subtopic (i.e. Language Mechanics)
- Directions, examples, and test questions

Skill Lessons

Skill lessons include sample questions and clues for mastering the skill. The questions are formatted as they generally appear in tests, whether the tests are standardized and nationally normed or state specific.

Skill Lessons Include

- Subtopic (i.e. Language Mechanics)
- Skill (i.e. Punctuation)
- Directions and examples
- Clues for completing the activity
- Practice questions

Use

This book can be used in a variety of ways, depending on the needs of the students. Some examples follow:

- Review the skills correlation on pages 8–10. Record the skills tested in your state and/or district on the blanks provided.

- Administer the comprehensive practice test for each content area. Have students use the sample answer sheet in order to simulate the actual testing experience. The tests for Reading, Language, and Math are multiple choice. Evaluate the results.

- Administer the sample test for the subtopics within the content area. Evaluate the results.

- Administer the specific skill lessons for those students needing additional practice with content. Evaluate the results.

- Use the skill lessons as independent work in centers, for homework, or as seatwork.

- Prepare an overhead transparency of skill lessons to be presented to a group of students. Use the transparency to model the skill and provide guided practice.

- Send home the Letter to Parent/Guardian found on page 7.

Clues for Getting Started

- Determine the structure for implementing *Spectrum Test Practice*. These questions may help guide you:

  - Do you want to assess the overall performance of your class in each academic area? If so, reproduce the practice test and sample answer sheet for each area. Use the results to determine subtopics that need additional instruction and/or practice.

  - Do you already have information about the overall achievement of your students within each academic area? Do you need more information about their achievement within subtopics, such as Vocabulary within Reading? If so, reproduce the sample tests for the subtopics.

  - Do your students need additional practice with some of the specific skills that they will encounter on the standardized test? Do you need to know which students have mastered which skills? These skill lessons provide opportunities for instruction and practice.

- Go over the purpose of tests with your students. Describe the tests and the testing situation, explaining that the tests are often timed, that answers are recorded on a separate answer sheet, and that the questions cover material they have studied.

- Do some of the skill lessons together to help students develop strategies for selecting answers and for different types of questions. Use the "clues" for learning strategies for test taking.

- Make certain that students know how to mark a separate answer sheet. Use the practice test and answer sheet so that they are familiar with the process.

- Review the directions for each test. Identify key words that students must use to answer the questions. Do the sample test questions with the class.

- Remind students to answer each question, to budget their time so they can complete all the questions, and to apply strategies for determining answers.

Reduce the mystery of taking tests for your students. By using *Spectrum Test Practice*, you have the materials that show them what the tests will look like, what kinds of questions are on the tests, and ways to help them be more successful taking tests.

Note: Determine the structure that best fits your class. Many portions of these tests may need to be read to your students. Use the same procedure that is used on state or standardized tests to provide the best practice for your students.

Note: If you wish to time your students on a practice sheet, we suggest allowing 1.25 minutes per question for this grade level.

Dear Parent/Guardian:

We will be giving tests to measure your child's learning. These tests include questions that relate to the information your child is learning in school. The tests may be standardized and used throughout the nation, or they may be specific to our state. Regardless of the test, the results are used to measure student achievement.

Many students do not test well even though they know the material. They may not test well because of test anxiety or the mystery of taking tests. What will the test look like? What will some of the questions be? What happens if I do not do well?

To help your child do his/her best on the tests, we will be using some practice tests. These tests help your child learn what the tests will look like, what some of the questions might be, and ways to learn to take tests. These practice tests will be included as part of your child's homework.

You can help your child with this important part of learning. Below are some suggestions:

- Ask your child if he/she has homework.
- Provide a quiet place to work.
- Go over the work with your child.
- Use a timer to help your child learn to manage his/her time when taking tests.
- Tell your child he/she is doing a good job.
- Remind him/her to use the clues that are included in the lessons.

If your child is having difficulty with the tests, these ideas may be helpful:

- Review the examples.
- Skip the difficult questions and go back to them if there is time.
- Guess at those that you do not know.
- Answer all the questions.

By showing you are interested in how your child is doing, he/she will do even better in school. Enjoy this time with your child. Good luck with the practice tests.

Sincerely,

● **Grade 1**

Sample Standards	Spectrum Test Practice Gr. 1	*CAT Level for Gr. 1	**CTBS Level for Gr. 1	Other	Other	Other
Reading						
Word Analysis						
Recognizing Letters	X					
Recognizing Beginning, Medial, and Ending Sounds	X	X	X			
Recognizing Rhyming Words	X					
Recognizing Compound Words	X					
Recognizing Contractions						
Recognizing Sight Words	X	X	X			
Other						
Other						
Vocabulary						
Using Synonyms	X		X			
Using Antonyms	X					
Matching Pictures to Words	X	X	X			
Categorizing Words		X				
Using Context Clues	X	X	X			
Understanding Root Words						
Other						
Other						
Reading Comprehension						
Identifying Main Idea with Pictures	X	X	X			
Identifying Details	X	X	X			
Matching Pictures to Sentences	X	X	X			
Identifying Sequence of Events	X	X	X			
Making Predictions	X	X	X			
Identifying Character Traits/Feelings	X	X	X			
Distinguishing Between Reality and Fantasy	X					
Identifying Author's Purpose	X					
Reading Various Genre	X	X	X			
Other						
Other						
Language						
Mechanics						
Expression						
Using Correct Capitalization and Punctuation	X	X	X			
Determining Correct Usage	X	X	X			
Recognizing Sentences	X		X			
Recognizing Paragraphs	X	X	X			
Other						
Other						

* Terra Nova CAT™   ©2001 CTB/McGraw-Hill
** Terra Nova CTBS®   ©1997 CTB/McGraw-Hill

Grade 1

Sample Standards	Spectrum Test Practice Gr. 1	*CAT Level for Gr. 1	**CTBS Level for Gr. 1	Other	Other	Other
Spelling						
Identifying Correct Spelling	X					
Identifying Incorrect Spelling	X					
Other						
Other						
Study Skills						
Using Book Parts*	X					
Other						
Math						
Concepts						
Numeration						
Using Number Lines	X					
Using Numbers Up to 100	X		X			
Ordering and Comparing Whole Numbers	X	X	X			
Using Place Value	X		X			
Other						
Other						
Algebra						
Recognizing Patterns with Pictures	X	X	X			
Extending Number Patterns	X	X	X			
Using Number Sentences	X		X			
Using Symbols To Represent Numbers	X					
Other						
Other						
Fractions and Decimals						
Recognizing Fractions from Pictures	X					
Other						
Other						
Computation						
Whole Numbers						
Demonstrating Mastery of Addition Facts to 20	X	X	X			
Solving Two-Digit Addition and Subtraction Problems Without Regrouping	X	X	X			
Other						
Other						
Probability						
Collecting Data						
Other						

* Terra Nova CAT™ ©2001 CTB/McGraw-Hill
** Terra Nova CTBS® ©1997 CTB/McGraw-Hill

● **Grade 1**

Sample Standards

	Spectrum Test Practice Gr. 1	*CAT Level for Gr. 1	**CTBS Level for Gr. 1	Other	Other	Other
Applications						
Geometry						
Identifying Shapes	X		X			
Identifying Lines of Symmetry	X		X			
Identifying Congruent Figures	X	X	X			
Other						
Other						
Measurement						
Using Standard and Non-Standard Measures	X	X	X			
Selecting Appropriate Measures	X					
Estimating	X					
Measuring to the Nearest Inch	X	X	X			
Reading Thermometers						
Telling Time to the Half Hour	X	X	X			
Recognizing Coins	X	X	X			
Other						
Other						
Problem Solving						
Selecting Appropriate Operations	X		X			
Using a Variety of Methods to Solve Problems, Including Graphs, Tables, and Charts	X	X	X			
Other						
Other						
Science						
Understanding Plant and Animal Attributes	X	X	X			
Understanding Properties of Materials	X	X	X			
Understanding the Water Cycle		X				
Understanding the Types of Matter	X	X	X			
Environment	X					
Seasons	X					
Other						
Social Studies						
Comparing the Past and Present in Their Community	X	X	X			
Identifying Rights and Responsibilities						
Explaining the Difference Between Maps and Globes	X	X	X			
Locating Community on U.S. Maps		X	X			
Identifying the Basic Vocabulary of Economics		X	X			
Other						

* Terra Nova CAT™ ©2001 CTB/McGraw-Hill
** Terra Nova CTBS® ©1997 CTB/McGraw-Hill

READING: WORD ANALYSIS

Lesson 1: Letter Recognition

Directions: Look at the word your teacher reads. Mark the letter the word begins with. Example A is done for you. Practice with example B.

Examples

A. Which letter does the word **sand** begin with?

- (A) b
- (B) l
- (●) s
- (D) c

B. Which letter does the word **large** begin with?

- (F) p
- (G) q
- (H) m
- (J) l

 Clue If you are not sure which answer is correct, take your best guess. Eliminate answer choices you know are wrong.

● Practice

1. Which letter does the word **park** begin with?

- (A) v
- (B) w
- (C) b
- (D) p

2. Which letter does the word **dog** begin with?

- (F) d
- (G) b
- (H) y
- (J) o

3. Which letter does the word **nice** begin with?

- (A) s
- (B) n
- (C) u
- (D) k

4. Which letter does the word **talk** begin with?

- (F) j
- (G) f
- (H) t
- (J) l

STOP

Name _____   Date _____

READING: WORD ANALYSIS

● Lesson 2: Beginning Sounds

Directions: Look at the picture. Listen to your teacher read the word. Listen to your teacher read the words to the right of the picture. Mark the word with the same beginning sound as the picture. Practice with example A.

Example

A. desk

- Ⓐ chair
- Ⓑ den
- Ⓒ bat
- Ⓓ man

Clue Say the name of the picture to yourself. Listen closely to the word choices.

● Practice

1. rabbit

- Ⓐ man
- Ⓑ bike
- Ⓒ paper
- Ⓓ ring

3. bag

- Ⓐ vase
- Ⓑ top
- Ⓒ bell
- Ⓓ fish

2. mop

- Ⓕ miss
- Ⓖ hill
- Ⓗ clock
- Ⓙ win

4. tie

- Ⓕ tag
- Ⓖ girl
- Ⓗ shell
- Ⓙ pin

READING: WORD ANALYSIS

● Lesson 3: Ending Sounds

Directions: Listen to your teacher read all the words. Mark the word with the same ending sound as the first word. Practice with examples A and B.

Examples

A. make

- (A) cat
- (B) rock
- (C) worm
- (D) pen

B. hive

- (F) web
- (G) fun
- (H) glove
- (J) tip

 Clue Listen carefully to the ending sound of each word.

● Practice

1. star

- (A) mop
- (B) leaf
- (C) jar
- (D) five

2. leg

- (F) rug
- (G) gone
- (H) rich
- (J) grab

3. stew

- (A) net
- (B) wheel
- (C) barn
- (D) now

4. hit

- (F) dish
- (G) win
- (H) not
- (J) hear

5. bell

- (A) rest
- (B) hill
- (C) boat
- (D) cab

STOP

Name _____   Date_____

READING: WORD ANALYSIS

● **Lesson 4: Rhyming Words**

Directions: Listen to your teacher read the word. Choose the picture that rhymes with the word. Practice with example A.

Example

A. mop

(A)

(B)

(C)

Clue Look at the pictures. Say the words to yourself. Listen for the ending sound.

● **Practice**

1. dog

(A)

(B)

(C)

2. hat

(F)

(G)

(H)

3. rock

(A)

(B)

(C)

STOP

1-57768-721-3 *Spectrum Test Practice 1*

READING: WORD ANALYSIS

Lesson 5: Word Recognition

Directions: Listen to your teacher read the word. Notice the underlined part. Then listen as your teacher reads the word choices. Listen for the word with the same sound as the underlined part and mark it. Practice with examples A and B.

Examples

A. m<u>u</u>d
- (A) but
- (B) sock
- (C) shell
- (D) cat

B. p<u>ou</u>nd
- (F) snow
- (G) spent
- (H) loud
- (J) rider

Do numbers 1–4 the same way. You may ask your teacher to repeat an item after all of the problems have been read one time.

Practice

1. r<u>o</u>se
- (A) rule
- (B) bake
- (C) pony
- (D) nine

2. sp<u>oo</u>n
- (F) here
- (G) smooth
- (H) after
- (J) chip

3. p<u>ea</u>ch
- (A) quiet
- (B) push
- (C) last
- (D) need

4. r<u>i</u>de
- (F) miss
- (G) line
- (H) street
- (J) horse

READING: WORD ANALYSIS

● **Lesson 6: Vowel Sounds and Sight Words**

Directions: Listen as your teacher reads the question and says the name of the picture. Then listen as your teacher reads the word choices. Choose the best answer. Example A is done for you. Practice with example B.

Examples

A. **What word has the same vowel sound as the picture?**

 pen

Ⓑ spoon

ⓒ kite

Ⓓ chip

B. **What word rhymes with shell?**

Ⓕ smell

Ⓖ dog

Ⓗ rode

Ⓙ mile

 Clue Listen to all choices before you mark your answer.

● **Practice**

1. **What word has the same vowel sound as the picture?**

Ⓐ mouse

Ⓑ long

ⓒ tick

Ⓓ spoon

2. **What word has the same vowel sound as the picture?**

Ⓕ bead

Ⓖ hive

Ⓗ quilt

Ⓙ apple

3. **What word has the same vowel sound as might?**

Ⓐ pin

Ⓑ time

ⓒ from

Ⓓ soul

4. **What word rhymes with tough?**

Ⓕ crow

Ⓖ pool

Ⓗ puff

Ⓙ ton

STOP

READING: WORD ANALYSIS

● Lesson 7: Word Study

Directions: Listen as your teacher reads the word choices. Mark the word that is a compound word. Practice with example A.

Directions: Listen as your teacher reads the sentence and the word choices. One will fill in the blank. Mark your choice. Practice with example B.

Examples

A.
- (A) airplane
- (B) ringer
- (C) tune

B. The dog _____ its food.
- (F) eat
- (G) ate
- (H) eating

 Clue Listen carefully each time your teacher reads directions. The directions may change.

● Practice

1.
- (A) toolbox
- (B) kitchen
- (C) gate

2.
- (F) warning
- (G) flowerpot
- (H) glasses

3.
- (A) teacup
- (B) pencil
- (C) jumping

4. I am _____ than you.
- (F) big
- (G) bigger
- (H) biggest

5. I _____ books.
- (A) readed
- (B) reads
- (C) read

6. He _____ hot.
- (F) weren't
- (G) wasn't
- (H) won't

STOP

Name _____ Date _____

● **Directions:** Listen as your teacher reads the problems and answer choices. Mark the best answer. Practice with example A.

Example

A. **What picture starts with the same sound as nut?**

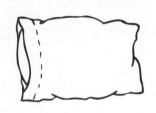  

(A)   (B)   (C)

1. **What picture begins with the same sound as cat?**

(A)   (B)   (C)

2. **What word begins with the same sound as the picture?**

(F) bat
(G) pig
(H) kite
(J) sun

3. **What letters show the beginning sound of the picture?**

(A) gl
(B) tr
(C) gr
(D) sl

4. **What word ends with the same sound as get?**

(F) tip
(G) sat
(H) run
(J) girl

5. **What word ends with the same sound as rash?**

(A) with
(B) luck
(C) push
(D) itch

GO ON

READING: WORD ANALYSIS
SAMPLE TEST (cont.)

● **Directions:** Listen as your teacher reads the words and answer choices. Look at the underlined part. Which word has the same sound as the underlined part? Practice with examples B and C.

Examples

B. ra<u>i</u>n

- (F) time
- (G) tan
- (H) name
- (J) spun

C. p<u>ie</u>

- (A) bake
- (B) pin
- (C) cup
- (D) ride

6. p<u>i</u>n

- (F) tip
- (G) had
- (H) shut
- (J) peel

7. ma<u>il</u>

- (A) cat
- (B) trade
- (C) kit
- (D) push

8. s<u>a</u>t

- (F) miss
- (G) pit
- (H) ban
- (J) same

9. sp<u>oo</u>n

- (A) touch
- (B) pool
- (C) tot
- (D) pad

10. m<u>ee</u>t

- (F) tick
- (G) piece
- (H) bun
- (J) stem

11. h<u>au</u>nt

- (A) paw
- (B) hat
- (C) hunt
- (D) stir

GO ON

● **Directions:** Listen as your teacher reads the words. Take away the first letter sound. Replace it with another sound. Mark the picture of the new word it makes.

12. bun

(F)   (G)   (H)

13. tail

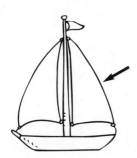   

(A)   (B)   (C)

● **Directions:** Choose the beginning sound that will make the word shown next to the picture.

14. ___ill

(F) m
(G) h
(H) p

16. ___ant

(F) pl
(G) st
(H) pr

15. ___ell

(A) ch
(B) th
(C) sh

STOP

READING: VOCABULARY

● **Lesson 8: Picture Vocabulary**

Directions: Listen to your teacher read the sentence. Choose the picture that finishes the sentence. Practice with example A.

Example

A. Bill drinks _____ .

Ⓐ

Ⓑ

Ⓒ

Clue   Listen carefully. Think about what you hear while you look at each picture.

● **Practice**

1. **I like to read _____ .**

Ⓐ

Ⓑ

Ⓒ

2. **The _____ ran fast.**

Ⓕ

Ⓖ

Ⓗ

3. **The baby _____ in her bed.**

Ⓐ

Ⓑ

Ⓒ

4. **The _____ rings.**

Ⓕ

Ⓖ

Ⓗ

STOP

Name _____   Date _____

● **Lesson 9: Word Reading**

Directions: Look at the picture. Listen as your teacher reads the word choices. Mark the word that matches the picture. Practice with examples A and B.

Examples

A.

- Ⓐ cat
- Ⓑ flower
- Ⓒ bird

B.

- Ⓕ sing
- Ⓖ bark
- Ⓗ read

Clue Listen to all answer choices before you choose.

● **Practice**

1. Ⓐ mom
   Ⓑ dog
   Ⓒ book

2. Ⓕ hug
   Ⓖ cry
   Ⓗ run

3. Ⓐ sit
   Ⓑ love
   Ⓒ eat

4. Ⓕ land
   Ⓖ shelf
   Ⓗ water

5. Ⓐ run
   Ⓑ skip
   Ⓒ swim

6. Ⓕ skin
   Ⓖ scales
   Ⓗ cloth

STOP

READING: VOCABULARY

Lesson 10: Word Meaning

Directions: Listen to your teacher read each phrase and the word choices. Mark the word that matches the phrase. Practice with examples A and B.

Examples

A. to move fast...
- (A) crawl
- (B) run
- (C) walk
- (D) sit

B. a cold thing...
- (F) ice
- (G) fire
- (H) sun
- (J) stove

 Clue Be sure about your answer.

Practice

1. a thing that flies...
- (A) pen
- (B) book
- (C) bird
- (D) cup

2. a thing that sings...
- (F) chair
- (G) girl
- (H) nest
- (J) paper

3. to drink a little...
- (A) spill
- (B) tip
- (C) sip
- (D) toss

4. to stay on top of water...
- (F) float
- (G) sink
- (H) pin
- (J) zip

5. noise a dog makes...
- (A) bark
- (B) purr
- (C) cut
- (D) land

6. a food...
- (F) wood
- (G) cart
- (H) apple
- (J) bed

 STOP

READING: VOCABULARY

● Lesson 11: Synonyms

Directions: Listen to your teacher read the sentence and word choices. Look at the underlined part. Mark the word that means about the same. Practice with examples A and B.

Examples

A. I was **sleepy**.

- (A) tired
- (B) running
- (C) tall
- (D) purple

B. Jill was in the **center**.

- (F) bowl
- (G) middle
- (H) end
- (J) side

Clue Think about what the sentence means.

● Practice

1. The car was **speedy**.
   - (A) better
   - (B) heavy
   - (C) fast
   - (D) able

2. She is **lovely**.
   - (F) pretty
   - (G) sharp
   - (H) sad
   - (J) near

3. The soup is **steaming**.
   - (A) soft
   - (B) spilling
   - (C) hot
   - (D) cold

4. Kida **washes** dishes.
   - (F) hides
   - (G) cuts
   - (H) sleeps
   - (J) cleans

5. It is a **small city**.
   - (A) house
   - (B) bus
   - (C) town
   - (D) road

6. We took a **boat** ride.
   - (F) car
   - (G) balloon
   - (H) ship
   - (J) bike

STOP

READING: VOCABULARY

Lesson 12: Antonyms

Directions: Listen to your teacher read the sentence and word choices. Look at the underlined part. Mark the word that means the opposite. Practice with examples A and B.

Examples

A. This is wet.

- Ⓐ big
- Ⓑ brown
- Ⓒ dry
- Ⓓ soaked

B. The rock is heavy.

- Ⓕ cold
- Ⓖ hard
- Ⓗ dirty
- Ⓙ light

 Clue Remember, the correct answer is the opposite of the underlined part.

Practice

1. The bear is tame.

- Ⓐ black
- Ⓑ wild
- Ⓒ hungry
- Ⓓ big

2. Susie whispered the secret.

- Ⓕ yelled
- Ⓖ tapped
- Ⓗ cried
- Ⓙ wrote

3. Why is it so little?

- Ⓐ loud
- Ⓑ bad
- Ⓒ big
- Ⓓ short

4. I run very fast.

- Ⓕ slow
- Ⓖ quick
- Ⓗ around
- Ⓙ loud

5. This is easy.

- Ⓐ less
- Ⓑ home
- Ⓒ simple
- Ⓓ hard

6. Jordan was sick.

- Ⓕ ill
- Ⓖ happy
- Ⓗ well
- Ⓙ tiny

STOP

READING: VOCABULARY

● **Lesson 13: Words in Context**

Directions: Listen to your teacher read the sentence and word choices. Choose the word that completes the sentence. Practice with examples A and B.

Examples

A. The _____ was green. It hopped far.

- (A) dog
- (B) rabbit
- (C) frog
- (D) boy

B. The _____ was long. It had 13 cars.

- (F) string
- (G) train
- (H) paper
- (J) hair

Clue When you think you hear the correct answer, put your finger next to it. Listen to all of the choices.

● **Practice**

1. Sam sat on the _____ . He soon fell asleep.

- (A) ice
- (B) chair
- (C) hammer
- (D) nail

2. The bee flew to its _____ . It went inside.

- (F) corner
- (G) cup
- (H) hive
- (J) honey

3. There are four _____ on the shelf. Tuti read them all.

- (A) cats
- (B) animals
- (C) suns
- (D) books

4. The joke was _____ . We all smiled.

- (F) funny
- (G) sad
- (H) blue
- (J) bread

STOP

Name _____ Date _____

READING: VOCABULARY
SAMPLE TEST

● **Directions:** Listen to your teacher read the phrase. Choose the picture that shows what the words mean. Practice with example A.

Example

A. A red fruit

Ⓐ

Ⓑ

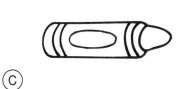
Ⓒ

Do numbers 1–4 the same way.

1. A good pet

Ⓐ

Ⓑ

Ⓒ

2. Summer fun

Ⓕ

Ⓖ

Ⓗ

3. A happy boy

Ⓐ

Ⓑ

Ⓒ

4. Something soft

Ⓕ

Ⓖ

Ⓗ

GO ON

Name _____   Date _____

● **Directions:** Look at the picture. Listen as your teacher reads the word choices. Mark the word that goes with the picture. Practice with examples B and C.

Examples

B.

Ⓕ head
Ⓖ arm
Ⓗ hand

C.

Ⓐ eat
Ⓑ walk
Ⓒ wear

Do numbers 5–10 the same way.

5.   Ⓐ frog
     Ⓑ turtle
     Ⓒ kitten

6.   Ⓕ throw
     Ⓖ read
     Ⓗ hold

7.   Ⓐ girl
     Ⓑ bear
     Ⓒ Santa

8.   Ⓕ read
     Ⓖ eat
     Ⓗ paint

9.   Ⓐ bag
     Ⓑ cup
     Ⓒ bowl

10.   Ⓕ snack
      Ⓖ ice cream
      Ⓗ mud

GO ON

Name _____   Date _____

READING: VOCABULARY
SAMPLE TEST (cont.)

Directions: Listen to your teacher read the sentence and word choices. Look at the underlined part. Mark the word that means about the same. Do numbers 11–13 the same way.

Directions: Listen to your teacher read the sentence and word choices. Look at the underlined part. Mark the word that is the opposite. Do numbers 14–16 the same way.

11. Brenda was <u>chilly</u>.
- (A) large
- (B) cold
- (C) small
- (D) done

14. Jetta <u>enjoys</u> music.
- (F) hates
- (G) likes
- (H) turns
- (J) eats

12. Bees are <u>insects</u>.
- (F) bugs
- (G) dish
- (H) hat
- (J) tire

15. The lion was <u>huge</u>.
- (A) hungry
- (B) sitting
- (C) small
- (D) fish

13. Levi made a <u>noise</u>.
- (A) flower
- (B) shell
- (C) sound
- (D) stone

16. A turtle is <u>slow</u>.
- (F) lazy
- (G) fun
- (H) tired
- (J) quick

GO ON

         1-57768-721-3 *Spectrum Test Practice 1*

READING: VOCABULARY
SAMPLE TEST (cont.)

Directions: Listen to your teacher read the phrases and word choices. Mark the word that matches the phrase. Do numbers 17–19 the same way.

17. **a thing we eat...**
- Ⓐ rope
- Ⓑ orange
- Ⓒ pail
- Ⓓ wheel

18. **a wild animal...**
- Ⓕ tiger
- Ⓖ butterfly
- Ⓗ fly
- Ⓙ pen

19. **a heavy thing...**
- Ⓐ feather
- Ⓑ sock
- Ⓒ truck
- Ⓓ balloon

Directions: Listen to your teacher read the sentences and word choices. Mark the word that completes the sentence. Do numbers 20–22 the same way.

20. **The show was great so we _____ .**
- Ⓕ clapped
- Ⓖ swam
- Ⓗ chewed
- Ⓙ blinked

21. **I ate the juicy _____ . It dripped.**
- Ⓐ bread
- Ⓑ stone
- Ⓒ peach
- Ⓓ book

22. **Some _____ fly south in the winter. It is warm.**
- Ⓕ bears
- Ⓖ girls
- Ⓗ trucks
- Ⓙ birds

STOP

READING: READING COMPREHENSION

● Lesson 14: Listening Comprehension

Directions: Listen to your teacher read each story. Choose the best answer for each question. Practice with example A.

Example

A. Henry Turtle was in a jam. He had been taking his walk when suddenly an owl landed on his head. What a surprise! What was on Henry's head?

Ⓐ

Ⓑ

Ⓒ

Clue Listen to each story. Think about what you hear, then mark your choice.

● Practice

1. Carol was going to ride her bike. She would go to the park. She asked Ray to go. His bike had a flat tire. What was wrong with Ray's bike?

Ⓐ

Ⓑ

Ⓒ

2. Carol and Ray walked to the park. They walked by the pond. They slid on the slide. They sat on the bench. On what did the children sit to rest?

Ⓕ

Ⓖ

Ⓗ

3. It started to rain. Carol and Ray ran home. They played with Carol's cat. They went to Ray's house. They fed his hamster. What did they play with at Carol's house?

Ⓐ

Ⓑ

Ⓒ

STOP

READING: READING COMPREHENSION

● **Lesson 15: Picture Comprehension**

Directions: Look at the picture. Listen to your teacher read the words next to the picture. Mark the choice that best describes the picture. Practice with example A.

Example

A.

(A) Butterflies have wings.
(B) I saw five butterflies.
(C) The plane was huge.

Clue The correct answer says the most about the picture.

● **Practice**

1.

(A) He reads books here.
(B) Three toys are by the chair.
(C) It was dark.

2.

(F) Tiger got a bath.
(G) It was muddy.
(H) I hate to take baths.

3.

(A) Tina has a cat.
(B) Buster chased the kitten.
(C) The cat is hungry.

4.

(F) I gave Mom a hug.
(G) He was sitting.
(H) Gifts are fun to get.

STOP

READING: READING COMPREHENSION

Lesson 16: Sentence Comprehension

Directions: Listen to your teacher read the sentence. Mark the picture that completes or matches the sentence. Practice with examples A and B.

Examples

A. **This is made of wood. You can write with it.**

 Ⓐ    Ⓑ   Ⓒ

B. **I ate a _____.**

Ⓕ book
Ⓖ cookie
Ⓗ mop

 Clue Listen to the sentence. Think before you make your choice.

● **Practice**

1. **This is hot. It helps things grow.**

 Ⓐ    Ⓑ   Ⓒ

2. **You smell with this. It is on your face.**

 Ⓕ   Ⓖ   Ⓗ

3. **This is my _____ .**

Ⓐ dog
Ⓑ school
Ⓒ lake

4. **There is a _____ in front of school.**

Ⓕ bike
Ⓖ frog
Ⓗ flag

 STOP

READING: READING COMPREHENSION

● Lesson 17: Fiction

Directions: Listen to your teacher read the story. Choose the best answers for the questions about the story. Practice with example A.

Example

The boy ran fast. He did not want to be late. Mom was making chicken. It was his favorite food.

A. **What was Mom making?**

- (A) shoes
- (B) chicken
- (C) puddles

 Clue **Listen carefully to the whole story.**

● Practice

Steve and his sister were playing. They were in the yard. A bird landed on the fence.

They watched the bird fly to the ground. It picked up some grass. Then it flew to a tree. Steve said the bird was making a nest.

1. **Who was with Steve?**

- (A) Steve's mother
- (B) Steve's sister
- (C) Steve's dog

2. **Where did the bird land?**

- (F) on the fence
- (G) on the roof
- (H) under the tree

STOP

READING: READING COMPREHENSION

Lesson 18: Fiction
Directions: Listen to your teacher read the story. Mark the best answers to the questions.

Get Warm

Brenda Butterfly was cold. She did not like it. She liked the sunny, warm weather. But it was autumn. "What can I do to get warm?"

Her friend Buddy knew what to do. "I think you should follow the birds. They fly to warm places in winter."

Brenda liked the idea. "That sounds great! Will you come with me, Buddy?"

They followed a flock of birds. It was a long trip. But it was so warm and sunny! Brenda and Buddy smiled. What a good idea!

There were many butterflies in this place. The flowers were colorful. Maybe Brenda and Buddy would stay.

1. **Brenda did not like _____ .**
   - (A) sunny weather
   - (B) being cold
   - (C) her friend Buddy

2. **What did Buddy think Brenda should do?**
   - (F) follow the birds
   - (G) light a fire
   - (H) get new coats

3. **Why should she follow the birds?**
   - (A) to find water
   - (B) to see snow
   - (C) to get to a warm place

4. **Two things Brenda and Buddy liked now were _____ .**
   - (F) their bird friends and fish
   - (G) colorful flowers and being warm
   - (H) flying far and the moon

═ READING: READING COMPREHENSION ═

● **Lesson 19: Nonfiction**

Directions: Listen to your teacher read the story. Choose the best answers to the questions about the story.

Spiders

Spiders are animals. The special name for their animal family is "arachnid." One spider is the tarantula. Another is the wolf spider. All spiders have eight legs. Most spiders spin webs of silk. The webs help the spider catch food. They eat mostly insects. Some spiders are big. There is one as big as a man's hand. Some spiders are very small. One spider is as small as the tip of a pin. This animal is helpful to people. Spiders eat harmful or pesky insects. They eat flies and mosquitoes.

1. **Spiders are _____ .**

   Ⓐ insects

   Ⓑ animals

   Ⓒ plants

2. **Spider webs are made of _____ .**

   Ⓕ silk

   Ⓖ rope

   Ⓗ wire

3. **Why are spiders helpful?**

   Ⓐ Spiders are big and small.

   Ⓑ A tarantula is a kind of spider.

   Ⓒ Spiders eat harmful insects.

4. **Why was this story written?**

   Ⓕ to tell about spiders

   Ⓖ to tell about mosquitoes

   Ⓗ to scare you

STOP

ame _____ Date_____

READING COMPREHENSION

Lesson 20: Nonfiction
Directions: Listen to your teacher read the story. Choose the best answers to the questions.

Statue of Liberty

The Statue of Liberty is in New York. It is a famous statue. People in France gave the United States the statue. This happened in 1884. They wanted to show their friendship.

It is one of the biggest statues ever made. The statue is made from copper. It shows a lady. She is dressed in a robe. She is wearing a crown. The lady is holding a torch and a tablet. A poet wrote a famous poem about the statue. It is on a bronze plaque. People read it when they visit.

Long ago, millions of immigrants, people coming to live in the United States, saw the statue. They felt like she welcomed them. It seemed like her torch was lighting the way to their new home. Millions of other people, called tourists, have also visited. They can climb up to the crown. They can see New York City. Many people around the world know about this great statue.

1. **Who gave the Statue of Liberty to the United States?**
   - (A) the people of France
   - (B) many immigrants
   - (C) the queen

2. **Why did they give the statue to the United States?**
   - (F) to make money
   - (G) so the United States would give them one
   - (H) to show friendship

3. **The statue is made from copper because _____ .**
   - (A) copper is ugly
   - (B) it is strong
   - (C) it smells nice

4. **Immigrants felt like the statue _____ .**
   - (F) worked like a flashlight
   - (G) welcomed them
   - (H) was too tall

Name _____ Date_____

READING: READING COMPREHENSION
SAMPLE TEST

● **Directions:** Listen to your teacher read the sentences. Mark the picture that best matches the sentences. Practice with example A. Do numbers 1–3 the same way.

Example

A. **This is my brother. He has glasses.**

 (A)    (B)    (C)

1. **Mother grew pretty flowers.**

 (A)    (B)    (C)

2. **It is fun at the park. We love to play.**

 (F)    (G)    (H)

3. **Kenny loves bears. They are his favorite animal.**

 (A)    (B)    (C)

GO ON

    1-57768-721-3 *Spectrum Test Practice 1*

READING: READING COMPREHENSION
SAMPLE TEST (cont.)

Directions: Listen to your teacher read the story and the questions. Choose the best answer for each question.

Kite Trouble

The wind was blowing. Inga wanted to fly a kite. It was sunny and warm. She went to the park. Jesse went with her. They ran all the way to the park.

Inga and Jesse got ready. Inga held the kite. Then she held the string. A big wind blew the kite high. Inga ran. Jesse wanted to try. When she stopped running, he asked Inga. Inga gave him the string. A big wind came. The string slipped. The kite went very high. The kite was caught in the tree. Inga and Jesse started to cry. They walked home. Maybe Daddy could help.

4. What did Inga want to do?

- (F) run with Jesse
- (G) fly a kite
- (H) play in the sun

5. What kind of weather was it?

- (A) sunny and warm
- (B) cold and windy
- (C) snowing

6. How did the kite get caught in the tree?

- (F) Daddy put it there.
- (G) Inga ran into the tree.
- (H) A big wind blew it there.

7. Why did Inga and Jesse cry?

- (A) The kite was in the tree.
- (B) It started to rain.
- (C) Jacob broke the kite string.

GO ON

READING: READING COMPREHENSION
SAMPLE TEST (cont.)

● **Directions:** Listen to your teacher read the story and questions. Mark the best answer for the questions.

Apples

Apples grow best where there are four seasons in the year. In the spring, apple trees will have white flowers and small green leaves in their branches. Then the flowers drop off. Tiny green apples start to grow as the weather gets warm. In the summer, the tree branches fill with small apples that grow and grow. In the fall, the big apples are ready to be picked. Leaves start to drop off the branches. In the winter, the apple tree will rest. It does not grow any leaves or apples. It is getting ready to grow blossoms and apples again in the spring.

8. **What grows on the apple tree branches first?**

   F apples
   G bee hives
   H flowers and leaves

9. **In what season do the apples grow and grow?**

   A fall
   B summer
   C winter

10. **What happens to apple trees in the winter?**

   F They rest.
   G They grow very tall.
   H Farmers cut them down.

11. **Why was this story written?**

   A to tell about winter
   B to tell about farming
   C to tell about apples

1-57768-721-3 Spectrum Test Practice 1

━━ ANSWER SHEET ━━

Part 1: WORD ANALYSIS

A (A)(B)(C)(D)
1 (A)(B)(C)(D)
2 (F)(G)(H)(J)
3 (A)(B)(C)(D)
4 (F)(G)(H)(J)

B (F)(G)(H)
C (A)(B)(C)
5 (A)(B)(C)(D)
6 (F)(G)(H)
7 (A)(B)(C)

8 (F)(G)(H)
9 (A)(B)(C)
D (F)(G)(H)
10 (F)(G)(H)
11 (A)(B)(C)

12 (F)(G)(H)
13 (A)(B)(C)
14 (F)(G)(H)
15 (A)(B)(C)

E (A)(B)(C)
F (F)(G)(H)
16 (F)(G)(H)
17 (A)(B)(C)

18 (F)(G)(H)
19 (A)(B)(C)

Part 2: VOCABULARY

A (A)(B)(C)
1 (A)(B)(C)
2 (F)(G)(H)
3 (A)(B)(C)
4 (F)(G)(H)

B (F)(G)(H)
C (A)(B)(C)
5 (A)(B)(C)
6 (F)(G)(H)
7 (A)(B)(C)

8 (F)(G)(H)
9 (A)(B)(C)
10 (F)(G)(H)
11 (A)(B)(C)
12 (F)(G)(H)

D (A)(B)(C)(D)
13 (A)(B)(C)(D)
14 (F)(G)(H)(J)
15 (A)(B)(C)(D)
16 (F)(G)(H)(J)

17 (A)(B)(C)(D)
18 (F)(G)(H)(J)
19 (A)(B)(C)(D)
20 (F)(G)(H)(J)
21 (A)(B)(C)(D)

22 (F)(G)(H)(J)

Part 3: READING COMPREHENSION

A (A)(B)(C)
1 (A)(B)(C)
2 (F)(G)(H)
B (F)(G)(H)
3 (A)(B)(C)

4 (F)(G)(H)
5 (A)(B)(C)
6 (F)(G)(H)
C (A)(B)(C)
7 (A)(B)(C)

8 (F)(G)(H)
9 (A)(B)(C)
10 (F)(G)(H)
D (F)(G)(H)
11 (A)(B)(C)

12 (F)(G)(H)
13 (A)(B)(C)
14 (F)(G)(H)
15 (A)(B)(C)
16 (F)(G)(H)

17 (A)(B)(C)
18 (F)(G)(H)
19 (A)(B)(C)
20 (F)(G)(H)
21 (A)(B)(C)

22 (F)(G)(H)
23 (A)(B)(C)
24 (F)(G)(H)
25 (A)(B)(C)
26 (F)(G)(H)

READING PRACTICE TEST

● **Part 1: Word Analysis**

Directions: Listen to your teacher read each question and the answer choices. Choose the best answer. Practice with example A. Do numbers 1–5 the same way.

Example

A. **Which letter does the word water begin with?**

Ⓐ t
Ⓑ v
Ⓒ m
Ⓓ w

1. **Which letter does the word heart begin with?**

Ⓐ p
Ⓑ b
Ⓒ d
Ⓓ h

2. **Which letter does the word take begin with?**

Ⓕ t
Ⓖ b
Ⓗ a
Ⓙ e

3. **Which letter does the word sunny begin with?**

Ⓐ c
Ⓑ s
Ⓒ y
Ⓓ l

4. **Which letter does the word bottle begin with?**

Ⓕ d
Ⓖ h
Ⓗ b
Ⓙ p

5. **Which letter does the word money begin with?**

Ⓐ m
Ⓑ n
Ⓒ w
Ⓓ j

STOP

READING PRACTICE TEST

Part 1: Word Analysis (cont.)

Directions: Listen closely as your teacher reads each question and the answer choices. Choose the word with the same beginning or ending sound. Practice with examples B and C. Do the same for numbers 6–9.

Examples

B. Which picture has the same beginning sound as **beet**?

C. Which word has the same ending sound as **slip**?

(A) truck
(B) sash
(C) map

---

6. Which picture has the same beginning sound as **cup**?

---

7. Which picture has the same ending sound as **Mike**?

---

8. Which word has the same beginning sound as **table**?

(F) cash
(G) shoot
(H) try

9. Which word has the same ending sound as **frog**?

(A) gray
(B) tag
(C) begin

READING PRACTICE TEST

● Part 1: Word Analysis (cont.)

Directions: Listen to your teacher say the words. Notice the underlined part. Listen as your teacher reads the word choices. Listen for the word with the same sound as the underlined part and mark it. Practice with example D. Do the same for numbers 10–15.

Example

D. w<u>i</u>g

    (F) time

    (G) swam

    (H) tip

10. p<u>a</u>t

    (F) from

    (G) mad

    (H) goes

11. m<u>i</u>ne

    (A) dime

    (B) into

    (C) hurt

12. p<u>u</u>mp

    (F) child

    (G) cutting

    (H) shark

13. sh<u>ou</u>t

    (A) loud

    (B) crow

    (C) pill

14. m<u>a</u>de

    (F) bank

    (G) puddle

    (H) line

15. b<u>e</u>g

    (A) mass

    (B) kelp

    (C) broke

STOP

READING PRACTICE TEST

● Part 1: Word Analysis (cont.)

Directions: Listen to your teacher read the words. Choose the picture that rhymes with the word. Practice with examples E and F. Do the same for numbers 16–19.

Examples

E. Which picture rhymes with **barn**?

Ⓐ   Ⓑ   Ⓒ

F. Which word rhymes with **tool**?

    Ⓕ   pool

    Ⓖ   book

    Ⓗ   lamp

---

16. Which picture rhymes with **dish**?

Ⓕ   Ⓖ   Ⓗ

---

17. Which picture rhymes with **car**?

---

18. Which word rhymes with **chance**?

    Ⓕ   dance

    Ⓖ   make

    Ⓗ   patch

19. Which word rhymes with **how**?

    Ⓐ   show

    Ⓑ   pow

    Ⓒ   zoom

Name _____ Date _____

READING PRACTICE TEST

Part 2: Vocabulary

Directions: Listen to your teacher read the group of words and answer choices. Choose the picture that matches the words. Practice with example A. Do the same for 1–4.

Example

A. Something to eat

(A)

(B)

(C)

1. Something that rings

(A)

(B)

(C)

2. Something to ride in

(F)

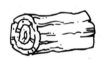
(G)

(H)

3. To get taller

(A) shrink

(B) grow

(C) empty

4. A place for clothes

(F) closet

(G) desk

(H) doghouse

STOP

1-57768-721-3 *Spectrum Test Practice 1*

READING PRACTICE TEST

Part 2: Vocabulary (cont.)

Directions: Look at the picture. Listen as your teacher reads the word choices. Mark the word that goes with the picture. Practice with examples B and C. Do the same for numbers 5–12.

Examples

B.

- (F) cap
- (G) box
- (H) jacket

C.

- (A) kick
- (B) throw
- (C) swing

5.

- (A) dance
- (B) run
- (C) sleep

6.

- (F) blanket
- (G) coat
- (H) hat

7.

- (A) one
- (B) two
- (C) three

8.

- (F) dog
- (G) girl
- (H) boy

9.

- (A) sledding
- (B) camping
- (C) shopping

10.

- (F) tent
- (G) car
- (H) van

11.

- (A) hot
- (B) snowing
- (C) raining

12.

- (F) sandcastle
- (G) toothpicks
- (H) jelly

STOP

READING PRACTICE TEST

● **Part 2: Vocabulary (cont.)**

Directions: Listen closely as your teacher reads the sentences and word choices. Choose the word that completes the sentence. Practice with example D. Do the same for numbers 13–16.

Example

D. **Camila _____ the phone.**

- (A) ringing
- (B) answered
- (C) went
- (D) shouted

13. **My mother drinks _____ .**
    - (A) tea
    - (B) nails
    - (C) watermelon
    - (D) sandwiches

14. **The _____ on the radio was loud.**
    - (F) sun
    - (G) water
    - (H) music
    - (J) computer

15. **Lucy walked all the way to the _____ .**
    - (A) over
    - (B) cut
    - (C) jar
    - (D) park

16. **Maisie sat on the _____ .**
    - (F) touch
    - (G) something
    - (H) bench
    - (J) large

STOP

Part 2: Vocabulary (cont.)

Directions: Listen closely as your teacher reads the sentences and word choices. Choose the answer that means the same or about the same as the underlined word for numbers 17–19.

Directions: Listen closely as your teacher reads the sentences and word choices. Choose the answer that means the opposite of the underlined word for numbers 20–22.

17. **Do you <u>like</u> watermelon?**

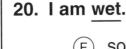

- Ⓐ make
- Ⓑ enjoy
- Ⓒ hate
- Ⓓ pat

18. **His ideas are always <u>great</u>!**

- Ⓕ wonderful
- Ⓖ crazy
- Ⓗ boring
- Ⓙ bunny

19. **<u>Listen</u> to the story.**

- Ⓐ taste
- Ⓑ hear
- Ⓒ look
- Ⓓ sit

20. **I am <u>wet</u>.**

- Ⓕ soaked
- Ⓖ dry
- Ⓗ yellow
- Ⓙ quiet

21. **Sammy is a <u>tiny</u> mouse.**

- Ⓐ large
- Ⓑ small
- Ⓒ friendly
- Ⓓ brown

22. **The glass is <u>full</u>.**

- Ⓕ mine
- Ⓖ Teri's
- Ⓗ empty
- Ⓙ broken

Name _____ Date_____

● **Part 3: Reading Comprehension**

Directions: Listen to your teacher read each story. Choose the best answer for the question. Practice with example A. Do the same for numbers 1–2.

Example

A. **Grandfather has a farm. He has many animals. He has pigs, chicks, and horses. He loves pigs the most. Which animal does Grandfather love the most?**

Ⓐ   Ⓑ    Ⓒ

1. **Katie packed her backpack. She took things to eat. She took things to drink. Which item wouldn't she put in her bag?**

Ⓐ   Ⓑ   Ⓒ

2. **Lilo was planting a garden. She had many tools. The tools helped her plant. Which picture shows something that Lilo didn't need when planting?**

Ⓕ   Ⓖ   Ⓗ

STOP

READING PRACTICE TEST

● Part 3: Reading Comprehension (cont.)

Directions: Listen to your teacher read the sentences. Look at the pictures. Choose the sentence that matches the picture. Practice with example B. Do 3–6 the same way.

Example

B.

(F) Todd ate cereal.

(G) I love my horse.

(H) The weather is nice.

3.

(A) The boat sunk.

(B) My pen does not work.

(C) Tanika swims everyday.

4.

(F) Lee gave him a car.

(G) My dad has a new watch.

(H) I see the clock.

5.

(A) We read together.

(B) I ran away from my brother.

(C) He plays the flute.

6.

(F) It was snowing.

(G) Parker was singing.

(H) I go to the library.

STOP

Name _____   Date _____

● **Part 3: Reading Comprehension (cont.)**

Directions: Listen to your teacher read the sentences. Match a picture to the sentences. Practice with example C. Do the same for numbers 7–10.

Example

C. **This floats high. Some people ride them.**

Ⓐ

Ⓑ

Ⓒ

---

7. **It was very cold. Mother said to wear these.**

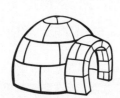
Ⓐ

Ⓑ

Ⓒ

---

8. **It was time. We had to get there fast!**

Ⓕ

Ⓖ

Ⓗ

---

9. **One boy is _____ .**

Ⓐ whispering

Ⓑ jumping

Ⓒ eating

10. **One boy is _____ .**

Ⓕ listening

Ⓖ awake

Ⓗ sleeping

STOP

READING PRACTICE TEST

● Part 3: Reading Comprehension (cont.)

Directions: Listen to your teacher read the story and the questions. Choose the best answer to the questions. Practice with example D. Do the same for numbers 11–14.

Example

Kida's party started at 2 o'clock. It was a pool party. People brought towels. They brought sunscreen.

D.   What kind of party did Kida have?

- (F)   birthday party
- (G)   pool party
- (H)   sunscreen party

The box was heavy. Simon needed help to move it. He asked Tom. He asked Kate. They went to help. The box was full. It had books in it. Tom and Kate decided to read. Simon sat down to read too. The box stayed.

11. What was in the box?
- (A)   Simon
- (B)   books
- (C)   boxes

12. How many people came to help Simon?
- (F)   1
- (G)   2
- (H)   3

13. What did Tom and Kate do?
- (A)   read books
- (B)   moved the box
- (C)   ran away

14. Why didn't they move the box?
- (F)   It was purple.
- (G)   They wanted to read.
- (H)   Kate went home.

READING PRACTICE TEST

● **Part 3: Reading Comprehension (cont.)**
Directions: Listen to your teacher read the story and the questions. Choose the best answer to the questions. Do the same for numbers 15–18.

Riley's Racer

"I want to make a car," Riley said to his father. "Will you help?"

"Yes! We can make a car. We need a plan. We need the tools. Then we will buy the things we need to make it."

Riley and his father drew a plan for the car. They decided on the size and color. Riley was so happy! It would be big! He could sit in it. It would roll down the hill in the yard. He would wear a helmet.

It took two weeks to make. They had fun. Mom took pictures. She even helped paint the car red. It was a fun family project.

15. **What did Riley want to make?**

   (A) tools

   (B) a car

   (C) pictures

16. **What did they do first?**

   (F) made a plan

   (G) painted

   (H) wore a helmet

17. **Why would Riley wear a helmet when riding in the car?**

   (A) to be safe

   (B) to hide his hair

   (C) to show his friend

18. **How did the family feel?**

   (F) sad

   (G) happy

   (H) angry

READING PRACTICE TEST

● **Part 3: Reading Comprehension (cont.)**

Directions: Listen to your teacher read the story and the questions. Choose the best answer to the question. Do the same for numbers 19–22.

Ship Shape

A ship is a very large boat. It can travel in the ocean. Some take trips across the whole ocean. Ships carry people and things from one place to another. They have people to work on them. These workers are called the crew.

A ship has many parts. The stern is the back of the ship. The bow is the front. On some ships masts hold the sails. The sails are like big sheets. They catch the wind and help ships go fast. Up on the mast might be a crow's nest. A sailor can sit there. He can watch the ocean.

Another important part is the helm. This is the ship's steering wheel. It can turn the ship to the left and right.

19. What is a ship?

(A) a train

(B) a very large boat

(C) a raft

20. Where do many ships travel?

(F) across the ocean

(G) in rivers

(H) to dark places

21. What do sails do?

(A) carry people

(B) cover people

(C) help the ship go

22. Why did the author write this story?

(F) to tell about sailors

(G) to tell about ships

(H) so people would buy boats

READING PRACTICE TEST

● **Part 3: Reading Comprehension (cont.)**

Directions: Listen to your teacher read the story and the questions. Choose the best answer to the question. Do the same for numbers 23–26.

What About Rabbits?

Rabbits are small animals. They have short, fluffy tails. Some have long ears that can hear very well. These ears can be floppy. Some also stick right up!

Rabbits eat all kinds of plants. They eat in fields. They eat in gardens. Some farmers do not like rabbits. They eat the vegetables farmers grow. Sometimes the rabbits eat young trees.

When a mother rabbit is having babies, she digs a hole. She puts in soft grass. She adds her own fur. This will keep the babies warm. She may have two to ten babies. Baby rabbits are called kits.

Some people have pet rabbits. They keep them in pens or cages. They might enter them in contests. Some pet rabbits can be trained to do tricks. Grains, vegetables, and grass are good foods for them.

23. What is this story mostly about?
- (A) rabbits
- (B) plants rabbits eat
- (C) farming

24. Why do some farmers not like rabbits?
- (F) They run on the grass.
- (G) They eat their trees and vegetables.
- (H) They make too much noise.

25. Where might pet rabbits sleep?
- (A) in a field
- (B) a pen or cage
- (C) under the blanket

26. What are good foods for pet rabbits?
- (F) vegetables and grass
- (G) hot dogs and candy
- (H) vegetables and meat

LANGUAGE: LISTENING

● **Lesson 1: Listening Skills**

Directions: Listen to your teacher read each story. Then choose the best answer for the question. Practice with example A.

Example

A. Mr. Turner is a teacher. He uses special tools. What is something that he uses?

(A)

(B)

(C)

Clue Listen carefully to the whole story and question. Then choose your answer.

● **Practice**

1. It was raining. I stayed in the house. I read books. Then I made cookies with Mother. It was a good day. What did I do first?

(A)

(B)

(C)

2. Marco likes to paint. He paints pictures of animals. At school he painted a picture of a parrot. The teacher liked it. The picture is hanging in the classroom. What animal did Marco paint at school?

(F)

(G)

(H)

3. Jamal went to the beach. He found three shells on Monday. He found five shells on Tuesday. On Wednesday, he found two more. How many shells did he find on Tuesday?

(A)

(B)

(C)

GO ON

Name _____ Date _____

LANGUAGE: LISTENING

● **Lesson 1: Listening Skills (cont.)**

4. The cat was meowing. She wanted to eat. Betty had no cat food! Lydia said she would go to the store. She would buy it. Maybe she would buy treats too. Where would Lydia go?

 (F)    (G)    (H)

5. Juan was playing. He has a soccer ball in the house. Mom said, "No kicking." But Juan kicked! The ball hit Mom's vase. It broke. Juan told Mom. They fixed it together. What broke?

(A)    (B)   (C)

6. Uncle Timothy is very tall. He plays a sport. He wears a blue and white shirt and shorts. He throws a ball. The people clap when it goes in the basket. He makes many points. Which sport does Uncle Timothy play?

(F)   (G)    (H)

STOP

Name _____   Date_____

LANGUAGE: LISTENING

● Lesson 2: Listening Skills
Directions: Listen to your teacher read the sentences. Then choose the best
answer to complete each story. Practice with examples A and B.

Examples

A. Dogs make good pets. Most are
friendly. They like to play. You
can train a dog. Dogs make
_____ .

- (A) good pets
- (B) dinner
- (C) plants grow

B. Tina was happy. It was her dad's
birthday. She made a card. Mom
made a cake. They would sing.
They would eat the _____ .

- (F) card
- (G) cake
- (H) birthday gift

● Practice

1. Rudy had one dollar. He used it
to buy a book. It was about
bugs. Rudy went home to read.
He sat by the tree. Rudy read
about _____ .

- (A) trees
- (B) dollars
- (C) bugs

2. They set up
camp. Sam put up
the tent. Kyle dug
a hole. Father
built a campfire. They cooked hot
dogs. Later they told stories. It
was time to sleep. Father told one
more story. The boys snored
loudly in the tent. The family set
up _____ .

- (F) a table
- (G) camp
- (H) the baseball game

3. Where did the boys sleep?

- (A) in the tent
- (B) next to the lake
- (C) in the kitchen

4. The phone rang. It was
Grandmother. She needed help.
Her cat ran away. Jack went on
his bike. The cat was up a tree.
She was meowing. Jack climbed
up the tree and got her. She was
happy to be down. Grandmother
was happy too. Grandmother
called _____ for help.

- (F) the cat
- (G) Jack
- (H) a dog

5. Why was she happy?

- (A) The cat was meowing.
- (B) Jack got the cat.
- (C) She took Jack's bike.

Name _____ Date_____

LANGUAGE: LISTENING

● **Lesson 3: Language Skills**

Directions: Listen to your teacher read the story. Mark the choice that best answers the question. Practice with example A.

Example

A.   **Mikkel plays baseball. What might he need to play?**

Ⓐ

Ⓑ

Ⓒ

Clue   If you are not sure which answer is correct, take your best guess.

● **Practice**

1.   **Tomas loves to watch planes. He goes to the airport. What does he use to see the planes?**

Ⓐ

Ⓑ

Ⓒ

2.   **The weather is hot. What does Petra need to keep cool?**

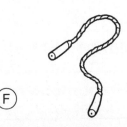
Ⓕ

Ⓖ

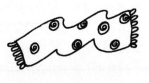
Ⓗ

3.   **Mark is going to the zoo. He will take some pictures. What will he take with him?**

Ⓐ

Ⓑ

Ⓒ

GO ON

Name _____ Date_____

LANGUAGE: LISTENING

Lesson 3: Language Skills (cont.)

4. It was fun at the beach. The girls swam for hours. What did they wear?

Ⓕ

Ⓖ

Ⓗ

5. Some animals are small. A mouse is small. Other animals are big. An elephant is big. Of the following pictures which shows the biggest animal?

Ⓐ

Ⓑ

Ⓒ

6. We will visit Aunt Tina. She lives very far away. We want to get there fast. How should we travel?

Ⓕ

Ⓖ

Ⓗ

7. Arthur built a clubhouse. It was in a tree. It was made of wood. He hung a sign. It said, "No girls can come in!" Who was upset about the sign?

Ⓐ

Ⓑ

Ⓒ

STOP

Name _____   Date _____

LANGUAGE: LISTENING
SAMPLE TEST

● **Directions:** Listen to your teacher read each story. Mark the best answer to the question. Practice with example A. Do numbers 1–6 the same way.

Example

A. Our neighbor has a garden. He grows vegetables. The vegetables are delicious. He grows corn and beans. He grows lettuce and tomatoes. What might be growing in the garden?

  (A)  (B)   (C)

1. Ethan likes to bake. He makes bread. The bread is good. He eats it in the morning. He toasts it. He puts jam on it. Sometimes he eats it plain. Which picture shows what Ethan makes?

 (A)   (B)  (C)

2. Todd looked in the box. He wanted a toy. The toy is soft. It has arms and legs. The toy is good to cuddle. His grandmother gave him this toy. What is Todd looking for in the box?

 (F)  (G)  (H)

3. Mr. Cortez wanted to paint. He went to the store. He got paint and brushes. He bought a tall ladder. He waited for a warm day. Then Mr. Cortez started to paint. What was he painting?

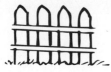 (A)  (B)   (C)

GO ON

1-57768-721-3 *Spectrum Test Practice*

LANGUAGE: LISTENING
SAMPLE TEST (cont.)

4. **Anita was ready. She was going to race. There were many people at the race. All the people were in a group. They ran fast. But Anita was the fastest! She won the race. What did Anita win?**

       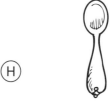

5. **Grandfather tells stories. They are about family. His family lived in the mountains. They lived near the woods. They had a farm and grew food. They also had many animals. Which animal might have been on the farm?**

6. **The weatherman said there would be thunder. He said there would be lightning. He said to bring an umbrella. Mother said to bring a jacket. What was the weather?**

GO ON

LANGUAGE: LISTENING
SAMPLE TEST (cont.)

● **Directions:** Listen to your teacher read each story. Listen to the answer choices. Mark the best answer to the question. Practice with examples B and C. Do 7–10 the same way.

Examples

B. Jesse had money. He needed milk. He ran fast. He wanted to get there quick. It would close soon. Where was Jesse going?

- (F) to the store
- (G) to school
- (H) to Grandmother's house

C. This is a good pet. Many people have this animal. It purrs. It meows. It chases mice. What kind of animal is it?

- (A) a kangaroo
- (B) a cat
- (C) a hamster

7. Penguins are birds. Most penguins live where it is cold and icy. They love to swim. They are fast swimmers. They have flippers that help them move fast. They can also slide! Sometimes they need to go fast. Swimming and sliding are two ways they go fast. Penguins slide on _____ .

- (A) bananas
- (B) ice
- (C) water

8. When penguins swim their flippers _____ .

- (F) help them move fast
- (G) turn yellow
- (H) turn into ice cubes

9. I open the door. I see balloons and streamers. I hear people laughing and talking. I see a big cake. There are candles on it. There is a big table. It has many boxes on it. The boxes are all colors and shapes. Someone sees me. Everyone says,

_____ .

- (A) "Go away!"
- (B) "Happy Birthday!"
- (C) "You are silly."

10. The colorful boxes are _____ .

- (F) for the trash
- (G) in the freezer
- (H) birthday gifts

STOP

Name _____ Date_____

Lesson 4: Capitalization

Directions: Listen to your teacher read each sentence. Which word in the sentence needs to be capitalized? If no more capital letters are needed, choose none. Practice with examples A and B.

Examples

A. My cat's name is bill.

- (A) Cat's
- (B) Name
- (C) Bill
- (D) None

B. the flower was pink and white.

- (F) The
- (G) Flower
- (H) White
- (J) None

Clue All sentences begin with capital letters. Names and place names begin with a capital letter.

Practice

1. School starts at 8:30.

- (A) Starts
- (B) At
- (C) 8:30
- (D) None

3. May i go to the park?

- (A) I
- (B) Go
- (C) Park
- (D) None

2. Her sister lives in michigan.

- (F) Sister
- (G) Lives
- (H) Michigan
- (J) None

4. We went on monday.

- (F) Went
- (G) On
- (H) Monday
- (J) None

STOP

LANGUAGE: LANGUAGE MECHANICS

● Lesson 5: Capitalization

Directions: Listen to your teacher read each story. Look at the underlined part. Think about how it should be written. Choose the best answer. Practice with example A. Do numbers 1–2 the same way.

Directions: Listen to your teacher read each sentence. Think about which word needs a capital letter. Choose the best answer. Practice with example B. Do numbers 3–5 the same way.

Examples

A. We got a new dog. We named her <u>cotton candy</u>. She is gold
     (A)
and brown.

  (A) cotton Candy
  (B) Cotton Candy
  (C) No change

B. Jack ran with tommy.

  (F) Ran
  (G) With
  (H) Tommy

The Race

We ran in a race. It was on

<u>Saturday, april 10</u>. We went down <u>main</u>
     (1)   (2)
<u>Street</u>. Then we turned on Jackson.

Timmy won!

1. How should the day of the race be written?

  (A) Saturday, April 10
  (B) saturday, April 10
  (C) No change

2. How should the name of the first street be written?

  (F) Main street
  (G) Main Street
  (H) No change

3. We start school on monday.

  (A) Start
  (B) School
  (C) Monday

4. we saw a bear.

  (F) We
  (G) Saw
  (H) Bear

5. She lives in washington.

  (A) Lives
  (B) In
  (C) Washington

STOP

LANGUAGE: LANGUAGE MECHANICS

Lesson 6: Punctuation

Directions: Listen to your teacher read the sentences. Some may need punctuation at the end. Choose the correct punctuation mark. If none is needed, mark None. Practice with examples A and B.

Examples

A. The horse ran

- (A) ?
- (B) .
- (C) None

B. How old are you?

- (F) .
- (G) !
- (H) None

 Clue Look for the missing mark that should go at the end of the sentences.

Practice

1. I like peanut butter

- (A) .
- (B) ?
- (C) None

2. Can Tish come over

- (F) .
- (G) ?
- (H) None

3. That is so huge

- (A) ?
- (B) !
- (C) None

4. Harvey caught a fish

- (F) .
- (G) ?
- (H) None

5. May I have more

- (A) .
- (B) ?
- (C) None

6. That is amazing

- (F) !
- (G) ?
- (H) None

 STOP

LANGUAGE: LANGUAGE MECHANICS

● Lesson 7: Punctuation

Directions: Listen to your teacher read each sentence. Does it need a punctuation mark? Choose the correct punctuation. Practice with example A. Do 1 and 2 the same way.

Directions: Listen to your teacher read the sentences and the questions. Choose the correct answer. Practice with example B. Do 3–4 the same way.

Examples

A. I read the book (A) It was long.

- (A) book?
- (B) book.
- (C) book!

B. This is a good cake

What punctuation mark comes after cake?

- (F) cake?
- (G) cake.
- (H) cake!

What is that I think it is a
_____
(1)
mouse! I am not scared
_____
(2)

1.

- (A) that.
- (B) that!
- (C) that?

2.

- (F) scared?
- (G) scared.
- (H) scared!

Time To Go

The party starts at 2 o'clock.

Oh no We will be late. Where are your
_____
(3)
shoes It is time to go.
_____
(4)

3. What punctuation mark comes after Oh no?

- (A) no.
- (B) no?
- (C) no!

4. What punctuation mark comes after Where are your shoes?

- (F) shoes?
- (G) shoes!
- (H) shoes.

STOP

LANGUAGE: LANGUAGE MECHANICS

Lesson 8: Capitalization and Punctuation

Directions: Listen to your teacher read the sentences. Look at each closely. Choose the sentence that has the correct punctuation and capitalization. Practice with examples A and B.

Examples

A.
- (A) I am tall.
- (B) John went to denver
- (C) today is Saturday.

B.
- (F) this blister hurts!
- (G) Tanya ran fastest
- (H) May I help?

 Clue Remember, you are looking for correct punctuation and capitalization.

Practice

1.
- (A) You are nice
- (B) george has short hair.
- (C) Andy is my friend.

2.
- (F) The Dog barked.
- (G) Where is Daddy?
- (H) Stop that yelling

3.
- (A) i went on Sunday.
- (B) Lydia left on Friday
- (C) Monday was hot!

4.
- (F) The Box is brown.
- (G) the baby was cute.
- (H) My pool is deep.

5.
- (A) Don't open that!
- (B) I hit the Ball?
- (C) Kyle found four leaves

6.
- (F) The joke was Funny!
- (G) We laughed.
- (H) May i have some water?

 STOP

Name _____   Date_____

LANGUAGE: LANGUAGE MECHANICS
SAMPLE TEST

● **Directions:** Listen to your teacher read each sentence. Which word in the sentence needs to be capitalized? If no more capital letters are needed, choose None. Practice with example A. Do numbers 1–6 the same way.

Example

A. **The phone on the desk rang.**

- (A) Phone
- (B) Desk
- (C) Rang
- (D) None

---

1. **My friend frank is twelve.**
    - (A) Friend
    - (B) Frank
    - (C) Twelve
    - (D) None

2. **her birthday is in May.**
    - (F) Her
    - (G) Birthday
    - (H) Is
    - (J) None

3. **Lottie painted the fence yesterday.**
    - (A) Painted
    - (B) Fence
    - (C) Yesterday
    - (D) None

4. **i filled the bag with candy.**
    - (F) I
    - (G) Bag
    - (H) Candy
    - (J) None

5. **Can brent come over today?**
    - (A) Brent
    - (B) Come
    - (C) Today
    - (D) None

6. **My sister goes shopping on Fridays.**
    - (F) Sister
    - (G) Goes
    - (H) Shopping
    - (J) None

GO ON

1-57768-721-3 *Spectrum Test Practice 1*

LANGUAGE: LANGUAGE MECHANICS
SAMPLE TEST (cont.)

Directions: Listen to your teacher read each story and the questions. Choose the best answer. Practice with examples B and C. Then do 7–10 the same way.

Examples

I wrote a Letter. It was to my uncle. I told him about Camp froggy.
      (B)   (C)

B. How should (B) be written?

- (F) a letter
- (G) A letter
- (H) The way it is.

C. How should (C) be written?

- (A) camp Froggy
- (B) Camp Froggy
- (C) The way it is.

Kittens for Free

There was a big sign. it said, "Free Kittens." I asked mom.
                      (1)   (2)

She said to ask Dad. It was fine with him. We named the kitten

Sonny. He liked to drink Milk.
 (3)   (4)

7. How should the first underlined part be written?

- (A) It Said,
- (B) It said,
- (C) The way it is.

8. How should the second underlined part be written?

- (F) Mom
- (G) MOM
- (H) The way it is.

9. How should the next underlined part be written?

- (A) Son Ny
- (B) sonny
- (C) The way it is.

10. How should the last underlined part be written?

- (F) milk
- (G) miLk
- (H) The way it is.

1-57768-721-3 *Spectrum Test Practice 1*

Name _____   Date _____

LANGUAGE: LANGUAGE MECHANICS
SAMPLE TEST (cont.)

● **Directions:** Listen to your teacher read each sentence. Choose the correct punctuation mark. If the sentence does not need punctuation, choose None. Practice with example D. Do 11–16 the same way.

Example

D. **The feather is soft**

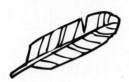

Ⓕ ?
Ⓖ .
Ⓗ None

11. **When did you get here**

Ⓐ .
Ⓑ ?
Ⓒ None

12. **That was super**

Ⓕ ?
Ⓖ !
Ⓗ None

13. **It smells like a flower**

Ⓐ ?
Ⓑ .
Ⓒ None

14. **Can it be fixed**

Ⓕ .
Ⓖ ?
Ⓗ None

15. **Wow, the Blue Jays won**

Ⓐ .
Ⓑ !
Ⓒ None

16. **My pencil broke**

Ⓕ ?
Ⓖ .
Ⓗ None

GO ON

1-57768-721-3 *Spectrum Test Practice 1*

LANGUAGE: LANGUAGE MECHANICS
SAMPLE TEST (cont.)

● Directions: Listen to your teacher read the story. Look at the underlined part. If it needs punctuation, choose the correct punctuation mark. Practice with example E. Do 17–20 the same way.

Example

The hot dog fell. I was very sad. <u>It was my dinner</u>
(E)

E. **What punctuation mark comes after It was my dinner?**

Ⓐ dinner?

Ⓑ dinner.

Ⓒ dinner!

Bats are flying mammals. <u>They can be big or small</u>
(17)

Some bats live in caves. Some live in old buildings. They

all like it dark. <u>Have you seen a bat</u> <u>I love bats</u> There
(18)   (19)

are bats in our barn. <u>They zoom over my head</u>
(20)

17. Ⓐ small.

Ⓑ small!

Ⓒ small?

18. Ⓕ bat?

Ⓖ bat!

Ⓗ bat.

19. Ⓐ bats!

Ⓑ bats?

Ⓒ bats.

20. Ⓕ head?

Ⓖ head.

Ⓗ head!

GO ON

 1-57768-721-3 Spectrum Test Practice 1

Name _____ Date _____

● **Directions:** Look at the sentences as your teacher reads. Choose the sentence that has the correct punctuation and capitalization. Practice with example F. Do the same with numbers 21–26.

Example

F.
  (F) I love winter Time.
  (G) Snowflakes can melt quickly.
  (H) December is a winter month?

21.
  (A) baby cats are Kittens.
  (B) Baby cows are calves.
  (C) A giraffe baby is a calf too

22.
  (F) Jumbo was an elephant.
  (G) children loved Jumbo.
  (H) Have you heard of Him?

23.
  (A) honeybees live in hives.
  (B) They make honey.
  (C) have you ever been stung!

24.
  (F) Apples are a fruit.
  (G) I love Potato Chips!
  (H) celery is crunchy.

25.
  (A) The soccer Ball flew!
  (B) It bounced high!
  (C) the team scored!

26.
  (F) dr. Conrad is nice.
  (G) She checks my teeth.
  (H) she is a dentist!

STOP

LANGUAGE: LANGUAGE EXPRESSION

Lesson 9: Usage

Directions: Listen to your teacher read the sentence and the word choices. Choose the best word to fill in the blank. Practice with examples A and B.

Examples

A. He _____ very well.

- (A) paint
- (B) painting
- (C) paints

B. The dog _____ .

- (F) was bark
- (G) were barking
- (H) was barking

 Clue Try each choice in the blank before deciding.

Practice

1. Harry is _____ this year than last year.

- (A) tall
- (B) taller
- (C) tallest

2. Jake and Winnie _____ .

- (F) swam together
- (G) is a light
- (H) faster than you

3. The fruit _____ juicy.

- (A) were
- (B) am
- (C) is

4. Her heart _____ fast.

- (F) beated
- (G) beating
- (H) beat

5. A caterpillar _____ leaves.

- (A) drink
- (B) eated
- (C) eats

6. _____ to the store.

- (F) The corner
- (G) We went
- (H) Anna

STOP

LANGUAGE: LANGUAGE EXPRESSION

● Lesson 10: Usage

Directions: Listen to your teacher read the sentence choices. Choose the sentence that is written correctly. Practice with examples A and B.

Examples

A.
- Ⓐ Them pies are good.
- Ⓑ That boys are taller.
- Ⓒ The cat purred.

B.
- Ⓕ It is beautifulest.
- Ⓖ We runned faster.
- Ⓗ It was thundering.

 Clue If you need to, repeat each choice to yourself.

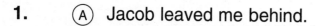

● Practice

1.
- Ⓐ Jacob leaved me behind.
- Ⓑ I paid for the pen.
- Ⓒ Can we went to the gym?

2.
- Ⓕ Last year we wented to the game.
- Ⓖ Today was fun.
- Ⓗ Tomorrow was busy.

3.
- Ⓐ Bob stand under the umbrella.
- Ⓑ We sits on the bench.
- Ⓒ The rain fell.

4.
- Ⓕ The sun rose.
- Ⓖ Raccoons is friendly animals.
- Ⓗ Deers isn't very big.

5.
- Ⓐ The rabbit jumping high.
- Ⓑ The new girl sit.
- Ⓒ London is a city.

6.
- Ⓕ She was so tires.
- Ⓖ Dinner was delicious.
- Ⓗ The ice melting quickly.

STOP

LANGUAGE: LANGUAGE EXPRESSION

Lesson 11: Pronouns

Directions: Listen to your teacher read the sentences and the word choices. Which pronoun makes sense in place of the underlined part? Mark your choice. Practice with examples A and B.

Examples

A. I saw Jim.

(A) he

(B) she

(C) him

B. We gave <u>the girls</u> candy.

(F) them

(G) it

(H) they

 The correct answer means the same as the underlined part.

Practice

1. **<u>Opal and I</u> were running.**

   (A) Them

   (B) We

   (C) They

2. **<u>Jason and Tami</u> are in trouble.**

   (F) It

   (G) They

   (H) Us

3. **I could not hear <u>my mother</u>.**

   (A) her

   (B) she

   (C) them

4. **Will you listen to <u>Mrs. Herts</u> when she sings?**

   (F) she

   (G) I

   (H) her

5. **<u>The sun</u> was very bright.**

   (A) His

   (B) It

   (C) Them

6. **He is as short as <u>Max</u>.**

   (F) he

   (G) they

   (H) him

LANGUAGE: LANGUAGE EXPRESSION

● Lesson 12: Sentences

Directions: Listen to your teacher read the sentences and the answer choices. Think about how the sentence could be turned into a question that makes sense. Choose the best answer. Practice with examples A and B.

Examples

A. I was early.

- (A) Early I was?
- (B) Was I early?
- (C) I early was?

B. The horse is racing.

- (F) Racing is the horse?
- (G) Is the horse racing?
- (H) Horse racing is the?

 Clue Say each answer choice to yourself.

● Practice

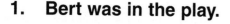

1. Bert was in the play.

- (A) In the play was Bert?
- (B) Was the play in Bert?
- (C) Was Bert in the play?

3. My name is Conrad.

- (A) Conrad my name is?
- (B) Is Conrad my name?
- (C) Name my Conrad is?

2. They will go skating.

- (F) Will they go skating?
- (G) Go skating will they?
- (H) Skating will they go?

4. The flower was in bloom.

- (F) Was the flower in bloom?
- (G) In bloom was the flower?
- (H) The flower in bloom was?

LANGUAGE: LANGUAGE EXPRESSION

● Lesson 13: Sentences

Directions: Listen to your teacher read these groups of words. Choose which group is a complete sentence. Practice with examples A and B.

Examples

A.
- Ⓐ To the store.
- Ⓑ The tree is tall.
- Ⓒ Won the race.

B.
- Ⓕ The butterfly.
- Ⓖ Sun rose.
- Ⓗ The moon is full.

 Clue Say each answer choice to yourself.

● Practice

1.
- Ⓐ Our yard.
- Ⓑ It rained all night.
- Ⓒ Jumped up.

2.
- Ⓕ Chip flew the kite high.
- Ⓖ Under the rock.
- Ⓗ Some people.

3.
- Ⓐ Phone number is.
- Ⓑ Bird nests.
- Ⓒ Paco has a new coat.

4.
- Ⓕ When was the?
- Ⓖ Was open all day.
- Ⓗ He picked the biggest one.

5.
- Ⓐ Read the.
- Ⓑ To the zoo.
- Ⓒ It snows in the winter.

6.
- Ⓕ Babies like rattles.
- Ⓖ Likes to sing.
- Ⓗ Fish and frogs.

STOP

LANGUAGE: LANGUAGE EXPRESSION

● **Lesson 14: Paragraphs**

Directions: A paragraph is a group of sentences all about the same idea. Listen to your teacher read the groups of sentences and the answer choices. Choose the sentence that best completes the paragraph. Practice together with example A.

Example

A. **It rained hard. There were many puddles. _____ .**

Ⓐ Birds built nests.

Ⓑ We splashed in the water.

Ⓒ The sun was hot.

 Clue The correct answer fits best with the other sentences.

● **Practice**

1. **Hanna sat down to read. She read a long time. _____ .**

   Ⓐ She finished the book.

   Ⓑ It was her brother's dog.

   Ⓒ The radio was loud.

2. **The family went on a trip. They were going far away. _____ .**

   Ⓕ They went on skates.

   Ⓖ They took an airplane.

   Ⓗ Kim did not like the apple.

3. **It was so dark. I looked up at the sky. _____ .**

   Ⓐ I ate a cookie.

   Ⓑ I saw many stars.

   Ⓒ The grass was cool.

4. **Vera is my sister. She is older than me. _____ .**

   Ⓕ My dog is black.

   Ⓖ She is also taller than me.

   Ⓗ Our cat purrs.

 STOP

Name _____   Date_____

LANGUAGE: LANGUAGE EXPRESSION
SAMPLE TEST

Directions: Listen to your teacher read the sentences and choose the word that best fills in the blank. Practice with example A.

Directions: Listen to your teacher read the sentences and choose the sentence that is written correctly. Practice with example B.

Examples

A. Betty _____ lots of books.

- (A) reads
- (B) readed
- (C) reading

B.
- (F) I lives by Kim.
- (G) Peter running to the corner.
- (H) It is very hot.

---

1. The _____ scored three points.
   - (A) team
   - (B) ball
   - (C) net

2. _____ were jumping rope.
   - (F) The trees
   - (G) Four girls
   - (H) Mrs. Connor

3. The _____ tasted great!
   - (A) car
   - (B) boat
   - (C) cake

4.
   - (F) They raking leaves.
   - (G) I loves her very much.
   - (H) We went to Tokyo.

5.
   - (A) Will Grandfather comes too?
   - (B) Uncle Torres is old.
   - (C) Mine hair is gray.

6.
   - (F) The pictures is ripped.
   - (G) We are freezing!
   - (H) The apple fallen.

GO ON

81

LANGUAGE: LANGUAGE EXPRESSION
SAMPLE TEST (cont.)

● **Directions:** Listen to your teacher read the sentences. As your teacher reads, look at the underlined part. Choose the pronoun that best replaces it. Practice with example C.

Directions: Listen to your teacher read the sentences. As you listen to your teacher, think about how the sentence sounds best as a question. Practice with example D.

Examples

C. **The plant** was green.
- (A) They
- (B) It
- (C) Them

D. **My hair is long.**
- (F) Hair long is my?
- (G) Is my hair long?
- (H) Long is my hair?

7. Tina bought <u>my mother</u> some candy.
- (A) she
- (B) them
- (C) her

8. <u>Lonny and I</u> are leaving.
- (F) We
- (G) Him
- (H) It

9. May I help <u>Mike</u> do that?
- (A) he
- (B) I
- (C) him

10. **This is a fun project.**
- (F) Is this a fun project?
- (G) A fun project this is?
- (H) A project fun this is?

11. **Kate's kite was stuck.**
- (A) Stuck was Kate's kite?
- (B) Was Kate's kite stuck?
- (C) Was stuck Kate's kite?

12. **My soda is gone.**
- (F) My soda gone is?
- (G) Gone is my soda?
- (H) Is my soda gone?

GO ON

LANGUAGE: LANGUAGE EXPRESSION
SAMPLE TEST (cont.)

Directions: Listen to your teacher read the sentences and choose the answer that is a complete sentence for numbers 13–15. Practice with example E.

Directions: Listen to your teacher read the sentences and choose the best sentence to complete the paragraph for numbers 16–18. Practice with example F.

Examples

E.
- (A) The tree lost its leaves.
- (B) In the closet.
- (C) A huge box.

F. Allie was crying. She had fallen. _____ .
- (F) She hurt her knee.
- (G) She ate cake.
- (H) It was yellow.

13.
- (A) Cutting the paper.
- (B) In the shed.
- (C) We all ate oranges.

14.
- (F) Yesterday.
- (G) Today was sunny.
- (H) Live in our barn.

15.
- (A) Tommy washes the car.
- (B) Cleaned the stove.
- (C) Did the laundry.

16. Grant and Ellie went fishing. Ellie had a bite! _____ .
- (F) Grant drank milk.
- (G) She caught a fish.
- (H) Birds fly south.

17. We do chores. I do the dishes. _____ .
- (A) The dog barks.
- (B) My dad likes coffee.
- (C) My brother puts the dishes away.

18. Dad was making popcorn. He burned it! _____ .
- (F) Mom opened a window.
- (G) Sparky ran in circles.
- (H) Can we go now?

STOP

LANGUAGE: SPELLING

● **Lesson 15: Spelling Skills**

Directions: Look at each word carefully. Which word is spelled **correctly**? Choose the best answer. Practice with examples A and B.

Examples

A.
- (A) car
- (B) cahr
- (C) carr

B.
- (F) bote
- (G) boat
- (H) boate

 If you are not sure which answer is correct, take your best guess. Eliminate answer choices you know are wrong.

● **Practice**

1.
- (A) darc
- (B) dahrk
- (C) dark

2.
- (F) furst
- (G) first
- (H) ferst

3.
- (A) summer
- (B) sumer
- (C) sammer

4.
- (F) perty
- (G) pretty
- (H) pretey

5.
- (A) depe
- (B) deep
- (C) deap

6.
- (F) papper
- (G) paiper
- (H) paper

STOP

LANGUAGE: SPELLING

● Lesson 16: Spelling Skills

Directions: Look at each group of words. Which word in each group is **not** spelled correctly? Practice with examples A and B.

Examples

A.
- (A) shell
- (B) smile
- (C) laike

B.
- (F) frunt
- (G) pin
- (H) game

 Clue If you are not sure which answer is correct, take your best guess.

● Practice

1.
- (A) brown
- (B) grean
- (C) white

2.
- (F) therd
- (G) second
- (H) first

3.
- (A) park
- (B) bank
- (C) trunck

4.
- (F) buzz
- (G) showd
- (H) talk

5.
- (A) kite
- (B) playng
- (C) balloon

6.
- (F) mahl
- (G) school
- (H) store

STOP

Name _____ Date _____

● **Directions:** Look at each word carefully. Which word is spelled correctly? Choose the best answer. Practice with examples A and B. Do numbers 1–6 the same way.

Examples

A.
- (A) whin
- (B) win
- (C) wen

B.
- (F) there
- (G) thair
- (H) thare

1.
- (A) somethin
- (B) sumthing
- (C) something

4.
- (F) fownd
- (G) foun
- (H) found

2.
- (F) right
- (G) ryte
- (H) riht

5.
- (A) teach
- (B) teech
- (C) teich

3.
- (A) nekst
- (B) next
- (C) nxt

6.
- (F) girl
- (G) gurl
- (H) grrl

GO ON

LANGUAGE: SPELLING SKILLS
SAMPLE TEST (cont.)

Directions: Look at the groups of words. Which word in each group is **not** spelled correctly? Practice with examples C and D. Do numbers 7–12 the same way.

Examples

C.
- (A) dri
- (B) pill
- (C) feel

D.
- (F) which
- (G) list
- (H) sutch

7.
- (A) toek
- (B) while
- (C) mother

8.
- (F) ten
- (G) tell
- (H) truble

9.
- (A) stop
- (B) gote
- (C) went

10.
- (F) again
- (G) that's
- (H) blak

11.
- (A) much
- (B) stood
- (C) ahr

12.
- (F) thenk
- (G) my
- (H) near

STOP

LANGUAGE: STUDY SKILLS

● **Lesson 17: Study Skills**

Directions: Look at the words as your teacher reads them. Choose the word that comes first in ABC order. Practice with example A.

Directions: Listen to your teacher read the sentences and the answer choices. Mark the best answer. Practice with example B.

Examples

A. **Which word comes first in ABC order?**

  (A) queen

  (B) bowl

  (C) pin

B. **If you need the meaning of a word, you look in a _____ .**

  (F) map

  (G) dictionary

  (H) pencil

 Stay with your first answer choice.

● **Practice**

1. (A) flew

    (B) zip

    (C) hill

2. (F) just

    (G) time

    (H) door

3. (A) head

    (B) yawn

    (C) line

4. **Steve needs directions to a city. Where might he look?**

    (F) a map

    (G) a dictionary

    (H) a bottle

5. **My report is about cooking. I talked to a _____ about it.**

    (A) police officer

    (B) chef

    (C) doctor

STOP

LANGUAGE: STUDY SKILLS

● Lesson 18: Study Skills

Directions: Read the table of contents with your teacher. It tells the names of chapters and what pages they are on in the book. Use it to answer the questions your teacher reads. Practice with example A.

Example

Table of Contents
Chapter 1—Rivers 3
Chapter 2—Lakes 6
Chapter 3—Seas 9
Chapter 4—Oceans 13

A. On which page will Maggie find information on oceans?

- (A) 6
- (B) 3
- (C) 13

 Clue Look at the table of contents with your teacher before starting the questions.

● Practice

Shelly wrote a report. It is about animals in the zoo. Here is her table of contents. Use it to answer the questions.

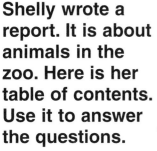

Table of Contents
Chapter 1—
Reptile House 2
Chapter 2—
Aquarium 4
Chapter 3—
Animals from North America 8
Chapter 4—
Animals from Africa 10

1. Which chapter tells about fish?

- (A) 2
- (B) 4
- (C) 3

2. How many chapters are about animals from Africa?

- (F) 4
- (G) 1
- (H) 10

3. What is another chapter Shelly could include?

- (A) Cars and Trucks
- (B) My Dog
- (C) Animals from South America

 STOP

LANGUAGE: STUDY SKILLS
SAMPLE TEST

● **Directions:** Listen to your teacher read the sentences and answer choices. Choose the best answer. Practice with examples A and B.

Examples

A. Which word comes first in ABC order?

- (A) keep
- (B) leap
- (C) bird

B. A table of contents shows _____ .

- (F) chapter names and pages
- (G) problems
- (H) definitions

For numbers 1–3, choose the word that comes first in ABC order.

1.
- (A) front
- (B) water
- (C) apple

2.
- (F) come
- (G) show
- (H) meet

3.
- (A) follow
- (B) three
- (C) bell

Will wrote a report about his grandfather's store. Use the table of contents at the top of the next column to help you answer questions 4 and 5.

Table of Contents

4. What page has information on making a shoe?
- (F) 8
- (G) 7
- (H) 1

5. Which chapter number tells about the types of shoes grandfather sells?
- (A) 1
- (B) 2
- (C) 3

STOP

ANSWER SHEET

STUDENT'S NAME

LAST | FIRST | MI

SCHOOL

TEACHER

FEMALE ○   MALE ○

BIRTH DATE

MONTH | DAY | YEAR

JAN ○
FEB ○
MAR ○
APR ○
MAY ○
JUN ○
JUL ○
AUG ○
SEP ○
OCT ○
NOV ○
DEC ○

DAY: ⓪①②③ ⓪①②③④⑤⑥⑦⑧⑨

YEAR: ⓪①②③④⑤⑥⑦⑧⑨ ⑤⑥⑦⑧⑨⓪

GRADE

① ② ③ ④ ⑤

Part 1: LISTENING

A ⒶⒷⒸ
1 ⒶⒷⒸ
2 ⒻⒼⒽ
3 ⒶⒷⒸ
4 ⒻⒼⒽ
5 ⒶⒷⒸ
6 ⒻⒼⒽ
7 ⒶⒷⒸ
B ⒻⒼⒽ
8 ⒻⒼⒽ
9 ⒶⒷⒸ
10 ⒻⒼⒽ

Part 2: LANGUAGE MECHANICS

A ⒶⒷⒸⒹ
B ⒻⒼⒽⒿ
1 ⒶⒷⒸⒹ
2 ⒻⒼⒽⒿ
3 ⒶⒷⒸⒹ
4 ⒻⒼⒽⒿ
C ⒶⒷⒸ
5 ⒶⒷⒸ
6 ⒻⒼⒽ
7 ⒶⒷⒸ
8 ⒻⒼⒽ
D ⒻⒼⒽ
E ⒶⒷⒸ
9 ⒶⒷⒸ
10 ⒻⒼⒽ
11 ⒶⒷⒸ
12 ⒻⒼⒽ
13 ⒶⒷⒸ
14 ⒻⒼⒽ
F ⒻⒼⒽ
G ⒶⒷⒸ
15 ⒶⒷⒸ
16 ⒻⒼⒽ
17 ⒶⒷⒸ
18 ⒻⒼⒽ
19 ⒶⒷⒸ
20 ⒻⒼⒽ

Part 3: LANGUAGE EXPRESSION

A ⒶⒷⒸ
B ⒻⒼⒽ
1 ⒶⒷⒸ
2 ⒻⒼⒽ
3 ⒶⒷⒸ
4 ⒻⒼⒽ
5 ⒶⒷⒸ
6 ⒻⒼⒽ
C ⒶⒷⒸ
D ⒻⒼⒽ
7 ⒶⒷⒸ
8 ⒻⒼⒽ
9 ⒶⒷⒸ
10 ⒻⒼⒽ
11 ⒶⒷⒸ

Part 4: SPELLING

A ⒶⒷⒸ
B ⒻⒼⒽ
1 ⒶⒷⒸ
2 ⒻⒼⒽ
3 ⒶⒷⒸ
4 ⒻⒼⒽ
5 ⒶⒷⒸ
6 ⒻⒼⒽ
C ⒶⒷⒸ
D ⒻⒼⒽ
7 ⒶⒷⒸ
8 ⒻⒼⒽ
9 ⒶⒷⒸ
10 ⒻⒼⒽ
11 ⒶⒷⒸ
12 ⒻⒼⒽ

Part 5: STUDY SKILLS

A ⒶⒷⒸ
1 ⒶⒷⒸ
2 ⒻⒼⒽ
3 ⒶⒷⒸ
4 ⒻⒼⒽ

Published by Spectrum. Copyright protected.   1-57768-721-3 Spectrum Test Practice 1

LANGUAGE PRACTICE TEST

● Part 1: Listening

Directions: Listen to your teacher read the story. Choose the best answer for each question. Practice with example A. Do the same for numbers 1–7.

Example

A. Teri knows how to make a sandwich. She can show us how. First, you need bread. Then you put it in the toaster. What is next?

 Ⓐ   Ⓑ    Ⓒ

1. There are many sounds. Sounds come from many things. Some are very loud. Others are very quiet. Which would make a very quiet sound?

Ⓐ    Ⓑ    Ⓒ

2. Vince wrote a report. It was about animals. Some animals are big. Other animals are small. He drew two pictures. One had big animals on it and one had small animals. Which animal would go on the picture of big animals?

Ⓕ    Ⓖ    Ⓗ

3. Maisie planted many seeds. She had a big garden. Later, Maisie picked good things to eat. Which picture shows something Maisie might leave in the garden?

Ⓐ    Ⓑ    Ⓒ

 GO ON

LANGUAGE PRACTICE TEST
Part 1: Listening (cont.)

4. The class worked very hard. They read many books. The prize is a pizza party. Mrs. Smith is going to buy the pizzas. The party is tomorrow. How do the students feel?

Ⓕ

Ⓖ

Ⓗ

5. Teddy looked up. He saw something in the sky. It was full of color. He wanted to catch it! He watched as it flew up. What did Teddy see?

Ⓐ

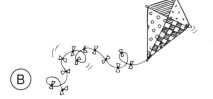
Ⓑ

Ⓒ

6. After dinner we had a treat. The treat was sweet. It was cool. We had to eat fast or it might melt. What was for dessert?

Ⓕ

Ⓖ

Ⓗ

7. Jessie had homework. She sat down in her room. She had everything she needed. Now she would start working. What won't she use to do her homework?

Ⓐ

Ⓑ

Ⓒ

STOP

LANGUAGE PRACTICE TEST

● **Part 1: Listening (cont.)**

Directions: Listen to your teacher read the story and answer choices. Choose the best answer to the question. Practice with example B. Do the same for numbers 8–10.

Example

B. Many people eat pizza. It can have many things on top. Some good things are cheese and meat. Some people like pizza with vegetables. Some even like it with fruit! Pizza needs to bake. Where would you bake a pizza?

(F) an oven
(G) a car
(H) a library

8. My family went to the beach. It was very hot. The sky was blue. We wore shorts. We collected shells. Mother brought lunch. We ate on the sand. Where did the family go?

(F) sky
(G) beach
(H) store

9. Jack saved his money. He had a bank. It was so heavy! He had a plan. He wanted a bike. It was blue and black. He knew it would go fast. What did Jack want to buy?

(A) a bank
(B) a blue shirt
(C) a bike

10. Mina had ten stickers. She wanted to share. She gave three to her brother. She gave three to her sister. Mother said she was a good girl. Mina gave her mother a sticker too! How many stickers did Mina give to her Mother?

(F) 1
(G) 3
(H) 0

94 1-57768-721-3 *Spectrum Test Practice*

LANGUAGE PRACTICE TEST

Part 2: Language Mechanics

Directions: Listen to your teacher read each sentence. Which word in the sentence needs to be capitalized? If no more capital letters are needed, choose None. Practice with examples A and B. Do the same for 1–4.

Examples

A. the rain fell.

   (A) The
   (B) Rain
   (C) Fell
   (D) None

B. I raked mr. Copper's leaves.

   (F) Raked
   (G) Mr.
   (H) Leaves
   (J) None

1. did you go to Andy's?

   (A) Did
   (B) You
   (C) Go
   (D) None

3. spiders spin pretty webs.

   (A) Spiders
   (B) Spin
   (C) Webs
   (D) None

2. They left on thursday morning.

   (F) Left
   (G) Thursday
   (H) Morning
   (J) None

4. the mouse loved cheese.

   (F) The
   (G) Mouse
   (H) Cheese
   (J) None

STOP

LANGUAGE PRACTICE TEST

● **Part 2: Language Mechanics (cont.)**

Directions: Listen to your teacher read each story. Look at the underlined part. Think about how it should be written. Choose the best answer. Practice with example C. Do numbers 5–8 the same way.

Example

C. **The trip was long. We were going to <u>aunt sue's</u> house.**

Ⓐ Aunt sue's
Ⓑ Aunt Sue's
Ⓒ The way it is.

Playing Soccer

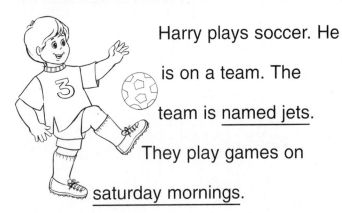

Harry plays soccer. He is on a team. The team is <u>named jets</u>. They play games on <u>saturday mornings</u>.

5. **Look at the first underlined part. How should it be written?**

Ⓐ named Jets
Ⓑ Named Jets
Ⓒ The way it is.

6. **Look at the second underlined part. How should it be written?**

Ⓕ satur Day mornings
Ⓖ Saturday mornings
Ⓗ The way it is.

School News

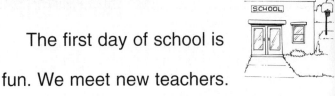

The first day of school is fun. We meet new teachers. We make new friends. My new teacher is tall. His name is <u>Mr. fuller</u>. He is <u>from Spain</u>.

7. **Look at the first underlined part. How should it be written?**

Ⓐ Mr. Fuller
Ⓑ mr. fuller
Ⓒ The way it is.

8. **Look at the second underlined part. How should it be written?**

Ⓕ From Spain
Ⓖ from spain
Ⓗ The way it is.

LANGUAGE PRACTICE TEST

● Part 2: Language Mechanics (cont.)

Directions: Listen to your teacher read the sentences. Some may need punctuation at the end. Choose the correct punctuation mark. If none is needed, mark None. Practice with examples D and E. Do the same for 9–14.

Examples

D. Where is the book

  Ⓕ .

  Ⓖ ?

  Ⓗ None

E. My name is Mary

  Ⓐ Mary?

  Ⓑ Mary.

  Ⓒ None

---

9. The screen went blank

  Ⓐ ?

  Ⓑ .

  Ⓒ None

10. Put the fire out

  Ⓕ ?

  Ⓖ !

  Ⓗ None

11. May I leave

  Ⓐ .

  Ⓑ ?

  Ⓒ None

12. Tilly was sick today

  Ⓕ today?

  Ⓖ today.

  Ⓗ today!

13. Is the milk sour

  Ⓐ sour?

  Ⓑ sour.

  Ⓒ sour!

14. He has a big smile

  Ⓕ smile.

  Ⓖ smile!

  Ⓗ smile?

STOP

LANGUAGE PRACTICE TEST

● **Part 2: Language Mechanics (cont.)**

Directions: Listen to your teacher read each sentence. Look at the words. Do they need capital letters or punctuation? Choose the sentence that is written correctly. Practice with examples F and G. Do the same with numbers 15–20.

Examples

F.			**G.**		
	(F)	my hands are blue		(A)	Sara ran backwards.
	(G)	I am cold.		(B)	the dog was sleeping
	(H)	i have a cold.		(C)	tim jumps high!

15.   (A) I have a red pen
      (B) kurt has black hair.
      (C) Nina dropped the spoon.

16.   (F) The paint is dry.
      (G) cora is ten.
      (H) Sela cannot Come?

17.   (A) Peggy was quiet
      (B) he wrote the letter.
      (C) Zack heard crying.

18.   (F) Jamal Won the Contest.
      (G) Blueberries are my favorite
      (H) Should we leave?

19.   (A) I will see you
      (B) can dennis type
      (C) He is so tall!

20.   (F) Give me a hug.
      (G) the soup tastes good?
      (H) I am Finished.

STOP

LANGUAGE PRACTICE TEST

Part 3: Language Expression

Directions: Listen to your teacher read the sentences and answer choices. Choose the word that best completes the sentence. Practice with example A.

Directions: Listen to your teacher read the answer choices. Choose the words that make up a sentence that is correctly written. Practice with example B.

Examples

A. Aunt Stella _____ good soup.

- (A) cooking
- (B) cook
- (C) cooks

B.
- (F) Now the group.
- (G) The middle part.
- (H) I ate the muffin.

---

1. The _____ was deep.

   - (A) rivers
   - (B) river
   - (C) rivering

2. Bess _____ horses well.

   - (F) drawing
   - (G) draws
   - (H) drawed

3. The shelf _____ .

   - (A) falling
   - (B) falled
   - (C) fell

4.
   - (F) Push the.
   - (G) Harvey rode the train.
   - (H) Cart fast.

5.
   - (A) Buddy was a.
   - (B) Big raindrops.
   - (C) It is cloudy.

6.
   - (F) Saturday will be fun!
   - (G) The picnic.
   - (H) Next week won't never be busy.

STOP

LANGUAGE PRACTICE TEST

● **Part 3: Language Expression (cont.)**

Directions: Listen to your teacher read the sentences and answer choices. Choose the best pronoun to replace the underlined words. Practice with example C.

Directions: Listen to your teacher read the sentences and answer choices. Choose the sentence that should come next. Practice with example D.

Examples

C. We went to see <u>Petra and Bill.</u>

   Ⓐ they
   Ⓑ them
   Ⓒ him

D. The dish broke. There was a mess. _____ .

   Ⓕ Mom was upset.
   Ⓖ Jimmy was sleeping.
   Ⓗ It is my birthday.

---

7. <u>Marion</u> had chicken pox.

   Ⓐ Her
   Ⓑ She
   Ⓒ They

8. <u>Hilda and I</u> were right!

   Ⓕ We
   Ⓖ Us
   Ⓗ Them

9. <u>My bike and skates</u> are broken.

   Ⓐ They
   Ⓑ Its
   Ⓒ I

10. Some food comes from animals. Milk comes from cows.

   _____ .

   Ⓕ Eggs come from chickens.
   Ⓖ Pumpkins grow fast.
   Ⓗ Pigs like mud.

11. Skunks are small mammals. They are black and white. They can give off a bad smell. Some skunks live in holes. _____ .

   Ⓐ Birds fly high.
   Ⓑ Skunks eat bugs, mice, and eggs.
   Ⓒ The snake was long.

STOP

LANGUAGE PRACTICE TEST

Part 4: Spelling

Directions: Look at the groups of words. Choose the word that is spelled **correctly**. Practice with examples A and B.

Examples

A.
- (A) jump
- (B) jamp
- (C) jhumpx

B.
- (F) feal
- (G) feil
- (H) feel

1.
- (A) parte
- (B) pahty
- (C) party

4.
- (F) hurrt
- (G) hurt
- (H) hert

2.
- (F) some
- (G) sume
- (H) soom

5.
- (A) whar
- (B) wair
- (C) where

3.
- (A) graet
- (B) grat
- (C) great

6.
- (F) wish
- (G) wesh
- (H) wich

STOP

LANGUAGE PRACTICE TEST

● Part 4: Spelling (cont.)

Directions: Look at the groups of words. Choose the word that is **not** spelled correctly. Practice with examples C and D.

Examples

C.		D.	
(A) will		(F) stand	
(B) them		(G) hant	
(C) triy		(H) pin	

7.
(A) way
(B) night
(C) thu

8.
(F) wuz
(G) nine
(H) stop

9.
(A) for
(B) fill
(C) sed

10.
(F) both
(G) werm
(H) very

11.
(A) pack
(B) liddle
(C) pass

12.
(F) all
(G) eye
(H) unter

STOP

LANGUAGE PRACTICE TEST

Part 5: Study Skills

Directions: Listen to your teacher read the story. Choose the best answer for each question. Practice with example A.

Example

Sonya Lee will write about puppies. She will write about how to care for them.

A. Who should Sonya Lee talk to about puppies?

- (A) a veterinarian
- (B) a mailman
- (C) a painter

Marnie wrote a story. It was about a trip. She went to a farm. The farm had many animals. She petted the rabbits. She milked a cow. She helped feed the pigs. The farmer showed her the field. It had corn growing in it. Marnie picked an ear of corn.

1. Marnie will put the animals in her report in ABC order. Which animal comes first?

- (A) rabbit
- (B) cow
- (C) pig

2. Who did Marnie talk to about the farm?

- (F) her teacher
- (G) farmer
- (H) Mr. Vera

Here is Marnie's table of contents.

Table of Contents

3. In which chapter will Marnie put the animals in ABC order?

- (A) 1
- (B) 2
- (C) 4

4. On what page does she talk about the surprise she saw on the farm?

- (F) 2
- (G) 4
- (H) 10

Name _____   Date_____

MATH: CONCEPTS

● **Lesson 1: Numeration**

Directions: Look at the pictures. Listen to your teacher read the question. Choose the best answer. Practice with example A.

Example

A. **Which bear is the biggest?**

(A)   (B)   (C)

 Clue Look at all answer choices before you mark the one you want.

● **Practice**

1. **Which player is third from the left?**

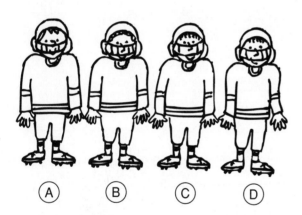

 (A)   (B)   (C)   (D)

2. **Which basket has the most socks?**

(F)   (G)   (H)

3. **How many blocks are there in all?**

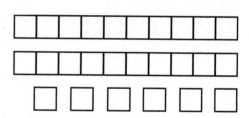

(A) 26
(B) 8
(C) 46
(D) 260

 GO ON

1-57768-721-3 *Spectrum Test Practice 1*

Lesson 1: Numeration (cont.)

4. **How many blocks are there in all?**

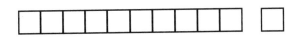

    (F) two

    (G) seven

    (H) three

    (J) eleven

5. **Which picture shows the carrot above the rabbit?**

    (A)

    (B)

    (C)

6. **Which number shows 4 tens and 5 ones?**

    (F) 405

    (G) 45

    (H) 9

    (J) 54

7. **Which number shows 10 tens and 2 ones?**

    (A) 10

    (B) 102

    (C) 120

    (D) 201

STOP

MATH: CONCEPTS

● **Lesson 2: Sequencing**

Directions: Look at the pictures. Listen to your teacher read the question. Choose the best answer. Practice with example A.

Example

A. How many candles are on the cake?

- Ⓐ 7
- Ⓑ 6
- Ⓒ 9

Clue If you are not sure which answer is correct, take your best guess.

● **Practice**

1. Which picture shows the bears smallest to largest?

Ⓐ

Ⓑ

Ⓒ

2. Count by ones. Which number comes after 15?

- Ⓕ 14
- Ⓖ 25
- Ⓗ 16
- Ⓙ 10

3. Which pattern needs the number 8 in the blank?

- Ⓐ 0, 1, 2, ____
- Ⓑ 2, 4, 6, ____
- Ⓒ 18, 28, 38, ____
- Ⓓ 3, 6, 9, ____

GO ON

MATH: CONCEPTS

Lesson 2: Sequencing (cont.)

4. **What is missing from this pattern?**

 (F)    (G)    (H)

5. **What is missing from this pattern?**

 (A)   (B)   (C)

6. **Look at the number line. Which number is more than 3 and less than 7?**

(F) 0
(G) 5
(H) 9

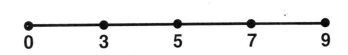

7. **Look at the number line. Which number is less than 5 and more than 3?**

(A) 4
(B) 2
(C) 8

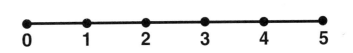

107   1-57768-721-3 *Spectrum Test Practice 1*

MATH: CONCEPTS

● Lesson 3: Number Concepts

Directions: Look at the pictures and numbers. Listen to your teacher read the question. Choose the best answer. Practice with example A.

Example

A. Which number shows eleven?

- Ⓐ 12
- Ⓑ 11
- Ⓒ 110
- Ⓓ 111

Clue Be sure the space you mark is for the answer you think is correct.

● Practice

1. Count the balls. How many are there?

- Ⓐ 7
- Ⓑ 6
- Ⓒ 5

2. How many dots are in the top part of the domino?

- Ⓕ 4
- Ⓖ 5
- Ⓗ 9

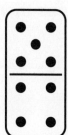

3. Look at the number in the box. Now look at the groups of apples. Which picture matches the number?

$$7$$

Ⓐ

Ⓑ

Ⓒ

GO ON

MATH: CONCEPTS

Lesson 3: Number Concepts (cont.)

4. Which number is the same as the word in the box?

(F) 7

(G) 55

(H) 5

5. Look at the number sentence in the box. Which number makes it true?

$$\square + 6 = 8$$

(A) 3

(B) 14

(C) 2

(D) 68

6. There were 5 books. Two fell off the table. How many were left?

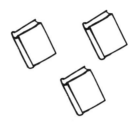

(F) $5 + 2 = 3$

(G) $5 - 2 = 3$

(H) $2 - 3 = 5$

7. Look at the number sentence. Which symbol makes it true?

$$13 \bigcirc 15$$

(A) >

(B) <

(C) =

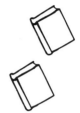

Name _____   Date_____

MATH: CONCEPTS

● **Lesson 4: Patterns and Place Values**

Directions: Look at the pictures. Listen to your teacher read the question. Choose the best answer for the question. Practice with example A.

Example

A. **Look at the pattern. Which one is the same?**

□ ○ ○ ○ □ ○ ○ ○ □ ○ ○

Ⓐ ○ ○ ○ □ □

Ⓑ □ ○ ○ □ ○ ○

Ⓒ □ ○ ○ □ ○

 Clue Sometimes it helps to say the pattern to yourself before making a choice.

● **Practice**

---

1. **Look at the pattern below. Which group has the same pattern?**

△ □ △ ○ △ □ △ ○ △ □ △ ○

Ⓐ △ □ △ ○ △ □ △ ○

Ⓑ △ △ △ □ ○ △ △ △

Ⓒ □ ○ □ ○ □ ○ ○

2. **Look at the pattern in the box. Which item will come next in the pattern?**

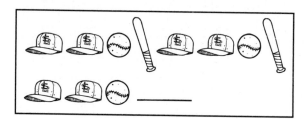

Ⓕ

Ⓖ

Ⓗ

GO ON ▶

MATH: CONCEPTS

Lesson 4: Patterns and Place Values (cont.)

3. Look at the number pattern in the box. If you count by 2s, what number should be in the blank?

2, __, 6, 8 10

Ⓐ 7

Ⓑ 4

Ⓒ 12

Ⓓ 11

4. Look at the blocks. How many tens are in the picture?

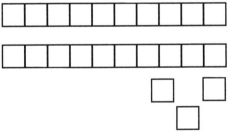

Ⓕ 3

Ⓖ 23

Ⓗ 2

Ⓙ 5

5. Look at the blocks. How many ones are in the picture?

Ⓐ 9

Ⓑ 8

Ⓒ 18

Ⓓ 43

6. How many tens are in the number 32?

Ⓕ 30

Ⓖ 2

Ⓗ 3

Ⓙ 5

STOP

Name _____ Date_____

MATH: CONCEPTS
SAMPLE TEST

● **Directions:** Look at the pictures. Listen to your teacher read the question. Choose the best answer. Practice with example A.

Example

A. **Which group has the most leaves?**

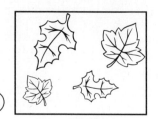 Ⓐ 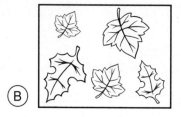 Ⓑ  Ⓒ

1. **Look at the number line. Which number shown is less than 5?**

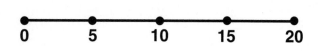

0   5   10   15   20

Ⓐ 0

Ⓑ 5

Ⓒ 20

Ⓓ 15

2. **Count the bubbles. How many bubbles are there all together?**

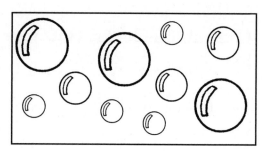

Ⓕ 9

Ⓖ 10

Ⓗ 11

Ⓙ 8

3. **Which numeral is thirty-two?**

Ⓐ 302

Ⓑ 5

Ⓒ 132

Ⓓ 32

GO ON

Published by Spectrum. Copyright protected.   1-57768-721-3 *Spectrum Test Practice 1*

MATH: CONCEPTS
SAMPLE TEST (cont.)

4. **Which puppy is second from the bowl?**

        (F)   (G)   (H)

---

5. **Look at the pattern. Which animal will come next?**

(A)   (B)    (C)

---

6. **Look at this number pattern. Which number goes in the blank?**

$$17, 18, 19, \_\_\_, 21, 22$$

(F) 16
(G) 20
(H) 10
(J) 23

---

7. **Look at the number in the box. Which group of boxes is the same number?**

7

(A)

(B)

(C)

GO ON

8. There are 3 flowers. Shelly planted 2 more. Which number sentence tells how many flowers there are?

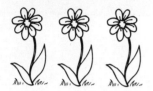 

F 3 − 2 = 1

G 3 + 2 = 5

H 3 + 5 = 8

J 8 − 2 = 6

9. How many tens and ones are there in 31?

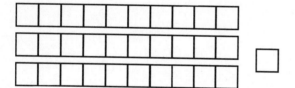

A 3 tens and 1 one

B 30 tens and 1 one

C 1 ten and 30 ones

D 10 tens and 3 ones

10. Look at the blocks. What number do they show?

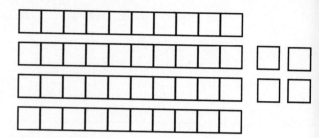

F 404

G 44

H 80

J 14

11. Look at the numbers in the boxes. Which one is in correct counting order?

A 2, 3, 4, 5

B 13, 14, 16, 17

C 12, 13, 15, 14,

GO ON

114

12. Look at the number pattern. Which number is missing?

$$2, 4, 6, 8, \underline{\quad}$$

(F) 1

(G) 10

(H) 18

(J) 9

13. Look at each group. Which does not show 5 items?

(A)

(B)

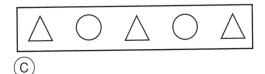
(C)

14. Look at the number line. Which number is between 3 and 7?

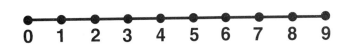
0 1 2 3 4 5 6 7 8 9

(F) 2

(G) 5

(H) 7

(J) 8

15. Look at the number sentence. Which symbol makes it true?

$$5 \bigcirc 2$$

(A) <

(B) >

(C) =

STOP

MATH: COMPUTATION

● Lesson 5: Addition

Directions: Solve each addition problem. Choose "None of these" if the right answer is not given. Practice with examples A and B.

Examples

A.
$$\begin{array}{r} 7 \\ +\ 1 \\ \hline \end{array}$$

- Ⓐ 9
- Ⓑ 8
- Ⓒ 6
- Ⓓ None of these

B.
$$\begin{array}{r} 1 \\ +\ 3 \\ \hline \end{array}$$

- Ⓕ 2
- Ⓖ 5
- Ⓗ 4
- Ⓙ None of these

 Clue If a problem is too difficult, skip it. Come back to it later if you have time.

● Practice

1.
$$\begin{array}{r} 6 \\ +\ 2 \\ \hline \end{array}$$

- Ⓐ 5
- Ⓑ 11
- Ⓒ 8
- Ⓓ None of these

3. $5 + 5 = \square$

- Ⓐ 5
- Ⓑ 55
- Ⓒ 10
- Ⓓ None of these

2.
$$\begin{array}{r} 2 \\ +\ 8 \\ \hline \end{array}$$

- Ⓕ 10
- Ⓖ 6
- Ⓗ 28
- Ⓙ None of these

4. $12 + 1 = \square$

- Ⓕ 4
- Ⓖ 13
- Ⓗ 22
- Ⓙ None of these

 GO ON

MATH: COMPUTATION

● Lesson 5: Addition (cont.)

5. $3 + 1 + 4 = \square$

(A) 8

(B) 0

(C) 13

(D) None of these

8. $\square + 11 = 16$

(F) 5

(G) 8

(H) 15

(J) None of these

6. $6 + 3 + 2 = \square$

(F) 65

(G) 11

(H) 5

(J) None of these

9.
$$\begin{array}{r} 3 \\ 8 \\ + 5 \\ \hline \end{array}$$

(A) 16

(B) 10

(C) 2

(D) None of these

7.
$$\begin{array}{r} 10 \\ 1 \\ + 2 \\ \hline \end{array}$$

(A) 103

(B) 7

(C) 13

(D) None of these

10.
$$\begin{array}{r} 13 \\ + 5 \\ \hline \end{array}$$

(F) 8

(G) 65

(H) 18

(J) None of these

STOP

MATH: COMPUTATION

● Lesson 6: Subtraction

Directions: Solve each subtraction problem. Choose "None of these" if the right answer is not given. Practice with examples A and B.

Examples

A.   5 − 2 =
- (A) 2
- (B) 3
- (C) 7
- (D) None of these

B.   7 − □ = 1
- (F) 7
- (G) 9
- (H) 6
- (J) None of these

Clue   Eliminate the answer choices that are bigger than the numbers being subtracted. These cannot be correct.

● Practice

1.   4 − 2 = □
- (A) 2
- (B) 6
- (C) 24
- (D) None of these

3.   10 − 2 = □
- (A) 8
- (B) 12
- (C) 56
- (D) None of these

2.
$$\begin{array}{r} 9 \\ -\ 4 \\ \hline \end{array}$$
- (F) 13
- (G) 93
- (H) 5
- (J) None of these

4.
$$\begin{array}{r} 11 \\ -\ 9 \\ \hline \end{array}$$
- (F) 20
- (G) 119
- (H) 2
- (J) None of these

GO ON

MATH: COMPUTATION

Lesson 6: Subtraction (cont.)

5. $6 - 1 = \square$

- (A) 4
- (B) 7
- (C) 5
- (D) None of these

6. $12 - 2 = \square$

- (F) 14
- (G) 10
- (H) 23
- (J) None of these

7.
$$\begin{array}{r} 9 \\ -\ 8 \\ \hline \end{array}$$

- (A) 17
- (B) 98
- (C) 89
- (D) None of these

8. $9 - 9 = \square$

- (F) 99
- (G) 0
- (H) 18
- (J) None of these

9.
$$\begin{array}{r} 8 \\ -\ 3 \\ \hline \end{array}$$

- (A) 5
- (B) 11
- (C) 65
- (D) None of these

10.
$$\begin{array}{r} 3 \\ -\ 2 \\ \hline \end{array}$$

- (F) 32
- (G) 203
- (H) 11
- (J) None of these

STOP

MATH: COMPUTATION
SAMPLE TEST

● **Directions:** Solve these addition and subtraction problems. Be sure to look closely at the sign. Choose "None of these" if the right answer is not given. Practice with examples A and B. Do numbers 1–12 the same way.

Examples

A. $9 + 1 = \square$
- (A) 10
- (B) 8
- (C) 19
- (D) None of these

B.
$$\begin{array}{r} 6 \\ -\ 4 \\ \hline \end{array}$$
- (F) 5
- (G) 64
- (H) 3
- (J) None of these

---

1. $2 + 5 = \square$
- (A) 3
- (B) 25
- (C) 7
- (D) None of these

2. $11 + 1 = \square$
- (F) 12
- (G) 111
- (H) 115
- (J) None of these

3. $6 - 6 = \square$
- (A) 15
- (B) 109
- (C) 0
- (D) None of these

4.
$$\begin{array}{r} 3 \\ +\ 3 \\ \hline \end{array}$$
- (F) 6
- (G) 32
- (H) 0
- (J) None of these

5.
$$\begin{array}{r} 7 \\ -\ 2 \\ \hline \end{array}$$
- (A) 8
- (B) 10
- (C) 5
- (D) None of these

6.
$$\begin{array}{r} 13 \\ -\ 0 \\ \hline \end{array}$$
- (F) 130
- (G) 4
- (H) 13
- (J) None of these

GO ON

7.
$$\begin{array}{r} 4 \\ -\ 1 \\ \hline \end{array}$$

- (A) 5
- (B) 3
- (C) 123
- (D) None of these

8. $8 + 2 = \square$

- (F) 12
- (G) 82
- (H) 16
- (J) None of these

9.
$$\begin{array}{r} 6 \\ +\ 4 \\ \hline \end{array}$$

- (A) 10
- (B) 9
- (C) 42
- (D) None of these

10. $4 + 1 + 0 = \square$

- (F) 415
- (G) 14
- (H) 5
- (J) None of these

11.
$$\begin{array}{r} 5 \\ -\ 4 \\ \hline \end{array}$$

- (A) 1
- (B) 9
- (C) 20
- (D) None of these

12. $9 + 8 = \square$

- (F) 720
- (G) 980
- (H) 17
- (J) None of these

STOP

Name _____ Date_____

━━━━━━━━━━ **MATH: APPLICATIONS** ━━━━━━

● Lesson 7: Geometry

Directions: Listen to your teacher read the problem. Look at the pictures. Choose the best answer for the question. Practice with example A.

Example

A. **Which one shows a triangle inside a square?**

 Clue Use key words and pictures to help you find the correct answer.

● Practice

1. **How many sides does a rectangle have?**

   (A) 3

   (B) 4

   (C) 5

   (D) 8

2. **Think about a triangle. How many sides does a triangle have?**

   (F) 3

   (G) 4

   (H) 5

   (J) 7

3. **Look at the shape. How many sides are there?**

   (A) 5

   (B) 8

   (C) 7

   (D) 4

4. **Look at the shapes in the box. How many circles do you count?**

   (F) 3

   (G) 6

   (H) 4

   (J) 0

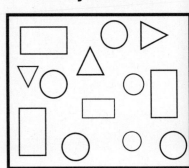

 GO ON

1-57768-721-3 *Spectrum Test Practice*

MATH: APPLICATIONS

● Lesson 7: Geometry (cont.)

5. Look at each group of shapes. Which one has the most stars?

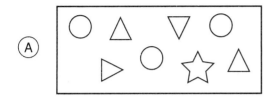

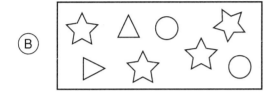

6. Which shape is not a triangle?

7. Look at the shape below. Look at the pictures. Which one is most like the shape below?

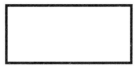

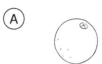

8. Look at the shape. Look at the pictures below. Which one is most like the shape below?

STOP

Name _____   Date _____

MATH: APPLICATIONS

● Lesson 8: Geometry

Directions: Listen to your teacher read the problem. Look at the pictures. Choose the best answer for the question. Practice with example A.

Example

A. Look at the shapes. When you fold one of them on the dotted line, the two sides will match perfectly. Which picture shows the shape that has two matching sides?

(A)   (B)   (C)

Clue Listen to your teacher read. Look at the shapes closely before answering.

● Practice

1. Look at the shapes. When you fold one of them on the dotted line, the two sides will match perfectly. Which picture shows the shape that has two matching sides?

(A)

(B)

(C)

2. Look at these shapes. Which one is different?

(F)   (G)    (H)

3. Look at the shapes in the box. How many have four sides?

(A) 2

(B) 4

(C) 5

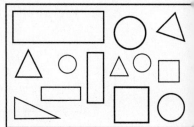

GO ON

Published by Spectrum. Copyright protected.   1-57768-721-3 *Spectrum Test Practice*

Name _____ Date _____

● Lesson 8: Geometry (cont.)

4. **Look at the shapes. Which has the most sides?**

(F)

(G)

(H)

5. **Which of these shapes is different from the others?**

(A)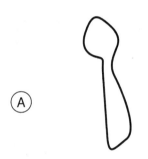

(B)

(C)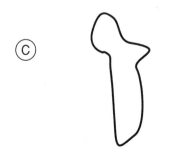

6. **Look at the shape below. Which item below is most like that shape?**

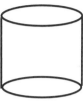

(F)

(G)

(H)

7. **Listen to this riddle. The star is inside the square. The star is not inside the circle. Which picture shows the answer to the riddle?**

(A)

(B)

(C)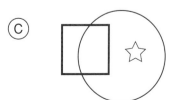

STOP

MATH: APPLICATIONS

● **Lesson 9: Measurement**

Directions: Listen to your teacher read the problems. Look at the pictures.
Choose the best answer for the question. Practice with example A.

Example

A. **Which tool would the doctor use to measure your temperature?**

Ⓐ

Ⓑ

Ⓒ

Clue Listen carefully to the problems as you look at the pictures. Then choose the correct answer.

● **Practice**

1. **Look at the fish and cat. Count how many fish long the cat is.**

   Ⓐ 4
   Ⓑ 3
   Ⓒ 5

2. **Look at the paper clips and pencil. Count how many paper clips long the pencil is.**

   Ⓕ 5
   Ⓖ 4
   Ⓗ 3

   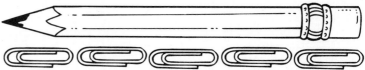

3. **Look at the ruler. About how many inches is the marker?**

   Ⓐ 3
   Ⓑ 5
   Ⓒ 6

   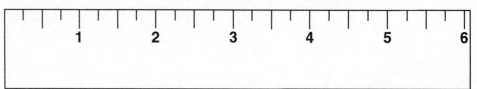

   GO ON

MATH: APPLICATIONS

● Lesson 9: Measurement (cont.)

4. **Look at the ruler. About how many inches is the pair of scissors?**

(F) 3

(G) 6

(H) 12

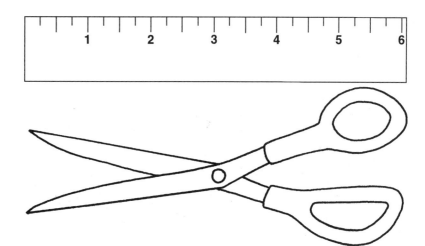

5. **Jacob wants to weigh himself. He would use a _____ .**

(A)

(B)

(C)

6. **Peter is cooking. What will he use to measure flour?**

(F)

(G)

(H)

7. **Lydia can eat half a pizza. Which picture shows how much pizza she can eat?**

(A)

(B)

(C)

STOP

Name _____ Date _____

MATH: APPLICATIONS

● Lesson 10: Measurement

Directions: Listen to your teacher read the questions. Look at the pictures. Choose the best answer for each question. Practice with example A.

Example

A. Which coin is a quarter?

(A)   (B)   (C)

 Clue Listen carefully to the question while you look at the pictures. Then make your answer choice.

● Practice

1. Which coin is a nickel?

(A)

(B)

(C)

2. Look at each group of coins. Which group has a penny and a dime in it?

(F)

(G)

(H)

3. How much is a penny worth?

(A) 10¢
(B) 1¢
(C) 50¢

4. How much is a dime worth?

(F) 25¢
(G) 10¢
(H) 5¢

GO ON

Name _____ Date _____

MATH: APPLICATIONS

Lesson 10: Measurement (cont.)

5. Look at the digital clocks. Which one shows the same time as the round clock face?

(A)  1:00

(B)  2:30

(C)  2:00

6. Look at the round clock faces. Which one shows the same time as the digital clock?

 4:30

(F)

(G)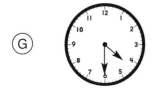

(H)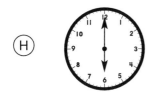

Look at this page of a calendar. Use it to answer questions 7 and 8.

SUN	MON	TUE	WED	THU	FRI	SAT
						MAY
1	2	3	4	5	6	7
8	9	10	11	12	13	14
15	16	17	18	19	20	21
22	23	24	25	26	27	28
29	30	31				

7. What day of the week is May 3?

(A) Tuesday
(B) Wednesday
(C) Friday

8. How many days are in two weeks?

(F) 7
(G) 5
(H) 14

STOP

MATH: APPLICATIONS

● Lesson 11: Problem Solving

Directions: Listen as your teacher reads the story. Choose the best answer for the question. Practice with example A.

Example

A. Trista had 3 candies. Mom gave her 2 more. How many does Trista have now?

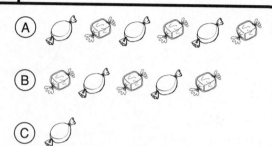

 Clue Listen carefully to the whole story and all of the answer choices.

● Practice

1. Jim had 5 ants in his ant farm. He caught 2 more. Then 3 ants crawled away. How many ants are left?

2. There were 8 cans of soda. Yani drank 5 cans. Lonny spilled 2 cans. How many are left?

3. Boris ran 2 miles yesterday and 1 mile today. He will run 1 mile tomorrow. How many miles will Boris run all together?

(A) 2

(B) 4

(C) 6

GO ON

MATH: APPLICATIONS

Lesson 11: Problem Solving (cont.)

CLASSROOM PETS

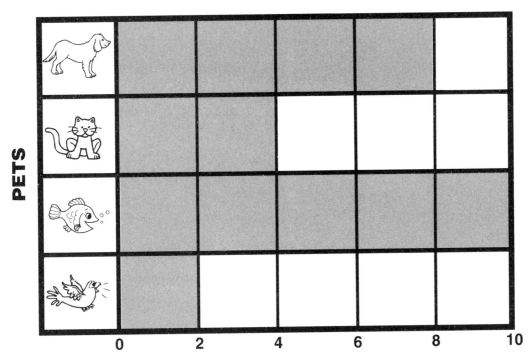

PETS

NUMBER OF STUDENTS

Look at the graph. It shows what pets the students have. Use it to answer questions 4– 6.

4. Which pet do 10 students have?
   - (F) fish
   - (G) dog
   - (H) cat

5. How many students have cats?
   - (A) 8
   - (B) 5
   - (C) 4

6. Which pet is the least popular?
   - (F) cats
   - (G) fish
   - (H) birds

7. Ian weighed 45 pounds. He gained one pound last year. He lost 3 pounds this year. How much does Ian weigh now?
   - (A) 45
   - (B) 43
   - (C) 42

131 1-57768-721-3 Spectrum Test Practice 1

MATH: APPLICATIONS

● Lesson 12: Problem Solving

Directions: Listen to your teacher read the story and the answer choices. Choose the best answer for the question. Practice with examples A and B.

Examples

A. He ate 9 apples. Then he ate 3 more. How many apples did he eat? Which number sentence shows how to find the answer?

- (A) $9 + 3 = 12$
- (B) $9 - 3 = 6$
- (C) $9 - 6 = 3$

B. The plant was 8 inches tall. It was 5 inches when Henry planted it. How much has the plant grown? Which number sentence shows how to find the answer?

- (F) $13 - 8 = 5$
- (G) $8 + 5 = 13$
- (H) $8 - 5 = 3$

 Clue Be sure to listen to the whole story. Eliminate the answer choices that you know are wrong.

● Practice

1. Jackie's dog had 6 puppies. How many dogs does Jackie have now?

- (A) $6 + 0 = 6$
- (B) $6 + 1 = 7$
- (C) $6 + 2 = 8$

2. I go to the movies. It costs $1.00 each time. I went Monday, Tuesday, and Saturday. How much did I spend all together?

- (F) $\$1.00 + \$1.00 + \$1.00 = \$33.00$
- (G) $\$1.00 + \$1.00 + \$1.00 = \$3.00$
- (H) $3 + \$1.00 = \$4.00$

3. Pepe lost 4 stickers this morning. He had 8 stickers last night. How many are left?

- (A) $4 + 8 = 12$
- (B) $8 - 4 = 4$
- (C) $4 - 4 = 0$

4. Mihn ran the race. She won 1 ribbon. If she had 7 ribbons already, how many does she have now?

- (F) $7 + 1 = 8$
- (G) $7 - 1 = 8$
- (H) $1 + 7 = 10$

GO ON

● **Lesson 12: Problem Solving (cont.)**

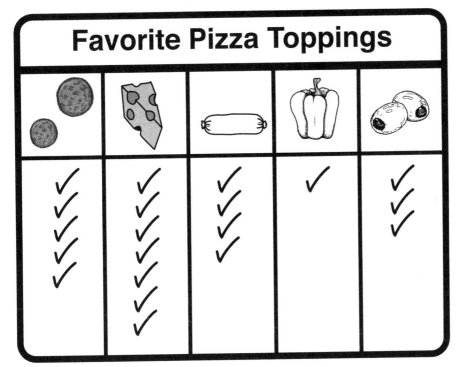

Favorite Pizza Toppings

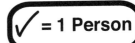 = 1 Person

Look at the graph. It shows which toppings people like on their pizza. Use it to answer numbers 5–8.

5. How many people like pepperoni?
   - Ⓐ 6
   - Ⓑ 5
   - Ⓒ 12

6. What is the topping most people like?
   - Ⓕ
   - Ⓖ
   - Ⓗ

7. How many people all together like cheese and pepperoni?
   - Ⓐ 12
   - Ⓑ 10
   - Ⓒ 6

8. What topping is the least favorite?
   - Ⓕ
   - Ⓖ
   - Ⓗ

 STOP

Name _____ Date _____

MATH: APPLICATIONS
SAMPLE TEST

● **Directions:** Listen to your teacher read the problem. Look at the pictures. Choose the best answer for the question. Practice with example A.

Example

A. Look at the shape below. Which of the shapes on the right matches it exactly?

Ⓐ

Ⓑ

Ⓒ

---

1. Look at the pictures. Which shows a rectangle with a triangle inside?

Ⓐ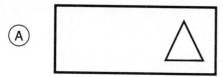

Ⓑ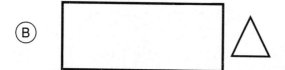

Ⓒ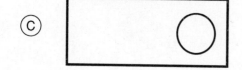

2. Look at these groups of shapes. Which group has 4 circles and 3 stars?

Ⓕ

Ⓖ

Ⓗ

3. How many sides does an octagon have?

Ⓐ 6

Ⓑ 8

Ⓒ 10

GO ON

1-57768-721-3 *Spectrum Test Practice 1*

MATH: APPLICATIONS
SAMPLE TEST (cont.)

4. Look at the ladder and the paper clips. How many paper clips long is the ladder?

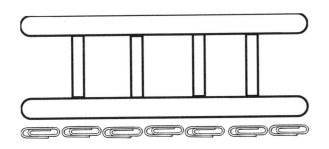

- (F) 6
- (G) 7
- (H) 12

5. Use the ruler. Which animal is the tallest?

6. Which tool would a mother use to weigh a baby?

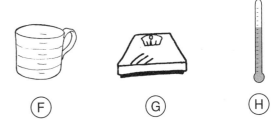

(F)   (G)   (H)

7. Tim, Tom, and Tina split a pie. They ate it all. Each got the same size piece. Which picture shows how they cut the pie?

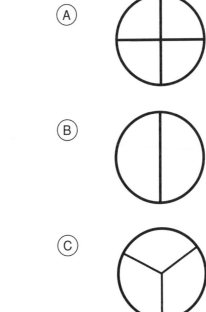

- (A)
- (B)
- (C)

GO ON

Name _____   Date_____

8. **Look at the clock face. Find the digital clock that says the same time.**

(F) 11:30

(G) 10:30

(H) 1:00

9. **Look at the digital clock. Find the clock face that says the same time.**

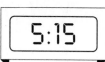

5:15

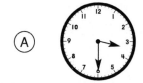

(A)

(B)

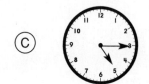

(C)

10. **How many days are in one week?**

(F) 5

(G) 7

(H) 10

11. **Justin had 4 coins. He had 13¢ all together. Which group of coins did he have?**

(A)

(B)

(C)

12. **Bart found 1 dime, 1 nickel, and 2 pennies. How much money did Bart find?**

(F) $1.12

(G) 17¢

(H) 12¢

GO ON

MATH: APPLICATIONS
SAMPLE TEST (cont.)

Mittens or Gloves?

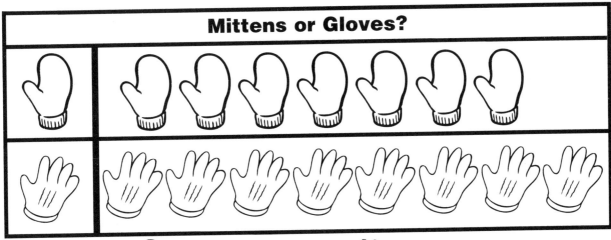

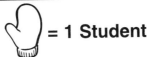 = 1 Student   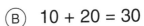 = 1 Student

Look at the graph. It shows how many people like to wear gloves or mittens. Use it to answer questions 13 and 14.

13. How many students like to wear mittens?

   (A) 8

   (B) 7

   (C) 15

14. How many people were asked to tell which they like best?

   (F) 15

   (G) 17

   (H) 8

15. Ned had 10 nails. He found 20 more. How many nails did Ned have?

   (A) $20 - 10 = 10$

   (B) $10 + 20 = 30$

   (C) $10 + 10 = 20$

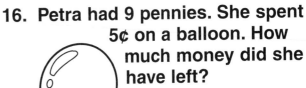

16. Petra had 9 pennies. She spent 5¢ on a balloon. How much money did she have left?

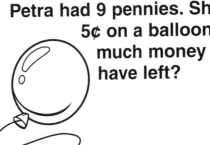

   (F) $9¢ + 5¢ = 14¢$

   (G) $9¢ - 5¢ = 4¢$

   (H) $5¢ + 9¢ = 32¢$

STOP

1-57768-721-3 *Spectrum Test Practice 1*

STUDENT'S NAME

LAST | **FIRST** | **MI**

SCHOOL

TEACHER

FEMALE ◯   MALE ◯

BIRTH DATE

MONTH	DAY	YEAR
JAN ◯	0 0	0
FEB ◯	1 1	1
MAR ◯	2 2	2
APR ◯	3 3	3
MAY ◯	4	4
JUN ◯	5	5 5
JUL ◯	6	6 6
AUG ◯	7	7 7
SEP ◯	8	8 8
OCT ◯	9	9 9
NOV ◯	0	
DEC ◯		

GRADE

① ② ③ ④ ⑤

Part 1: Concepts

A Ⓐ Ⓑ Ⓒ	**7** Ⓐ Ⓑ Ⓒ	**14** Ⓕ Ⓖ Ⓗ
1 Ⓐ Ⓑ Ⓒ	**8** Ⓕ Ⓖ Ⓗ	**15** Ⓐ Ⓑ Ⓒ
2 Ⓕ Ⓖ Ⓗ	**9** Ⓐ Ⓑ Ⓒ	
3 Ⓐ Ⓑ Ⓒ	**10** Ⓕ Ⓖ Ⓗ	
4 Ⓕ Ⓖ Ⓗ	**11** Ⓐ Ⓑ Ⓒ Ⓓ	
5 Ⓐ Ⓑ Ⓒ	**12** Ⓕ Ⓖ Ⓗ Ⓙ	
6 Ⓕ Ⓖ Ⓗ	**13** Ⓐ Ⓑ Ⓒ Ⓓ	

Part 2: Computation

A Ⓐ Ⓑ Ⓒ Ⓓ	**6** Ⓕ Ⓖ Ⓗ Ⓙ	**13** Ⓐ Ⓑ Ⓒ Ⓓ
B Ⓕ Ⓖ Ⓗ Ⓙ	**7** Ⓐ Ⓑ Ⓒ Ⓓ	**14** Ⓕ Ⓖ Ⓗ Ⓙ
1 Ⓐ Ⓑ Ⓒ Ⓓ	**8** Ⓕ Ⓖ Ⓗ Ⓙ	**15** Ⓐ Ⓑ Ⓒ Ⓓ
2 Ⓕ Ⓖ Ⓗ Ⓙ	**9** Ⓐ Ⓑ Ⓒ Ⓓ	**16** Ⓕ Ⓖ Ⓗ Ⓙ
3 Ⓐ Ⓑ Ⓒ Ⓓ	**10** Ⓕ Ⓖ Ⓗ Ⓙ	**17** Ⓐ Ⓑ Ⓒ Ⓓ
4 Ⓕ Ⓖ Ⓗ Ⓙ	**11** Ⓐ Ⓑ Ⓒ Ⓓ	**18** Ⓕ Ⓖ Ⓗ Ⓙ
5 Ⓐ Ⓑ Ⓒ Ⓓ	**12** Ⓕ Ⓖ Ⓗ Ⓙ	

Part 3: Applications

A Ⓐ Ⓑ Ⓒ	**7** Ⓐ Ⓑ Ⓒ	**14** Ⓕ Ⓖ Ⓗ
1 Ⓐ Ⓑ Ⓒ	**8** Ⓕ Ⓖ Ⓗ	**15** Ⓐ Ⓑ Ⓒ
2 Ⓕ Ⓖ Ⓗ	**9** Ⓐ Ⓑ Ⓒ	**16** Ⓕ Ⓖ Ⓗ
3 Ⓐ Ⓑ Ⓒ	**10** Ⓕ Ⓖ Ⓗ	
4 Ⓕ Ⓖ Ⓗ	**11** Ⓐ Ⓑ Ⓒ	
5 Ⓐ Ⓑ Ⓒ	**12** Ⓕ Ⓖ Ⓗ	
6 Ⓕ Ⓖ Ⓗ	**13** Ⓐ Ⓑ Ⓒ	

MATH PRACTICE TEST

Part 1: Concepts

Directions: Listen to your teacher read the question. Look at the pictures. Choose the best answer to the question. Practice together with example A. Do numbers 1–15 the same way.

Example

A. **Count how many stars are in this group.**

     (A) 8   (B) 9   (C) 7

1. **Look at the number in the box. Which group of blocks matches the number?**

14

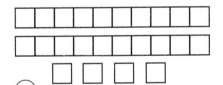 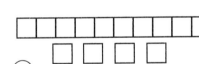 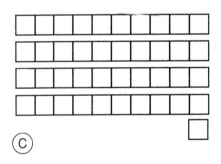

(A)   (B)   (C)

2. **Which vehicle is fourth in line from the left?**

                               (F)   (G)   (H)

3. **Which plant is the tallest?**

(A)   (B)   (C)   GO ON

MATH PRACTICE TEST
Part 1: Concepts (cont.)

4. Look at the numbers in the box. Put them in order, counting by ones. Which number will be last?

   | 15, 18, 14, 17, 16 |

   (F) 14

   (G) 16

   (H) 18

5. Think about counting by twos. Which number will go in the blank?

   | 4, 6, ___, 10, 12 |

   (A) 14

   (B) 8

   (C) 9

6. Look at the pattern. Which shape should be next?

   (F) circle

   (G) star

   (H) square

7. Look at the pattern. Which number should be next?

   | 0, 10, 20, ___, 40, 50 |

   (A) 25

   (B) 32

   (C) 30

8. **Look at the word in the box. How many letters do you count?**

calendar

- (F) 7
- (G) 16
- (H) 8

9. **Which group has the most fish?**

(A)

(B)

(C)

10. **Count the stars in the boxes. Which group of stars has seven?**

(F)

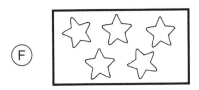

(G)

(H)

11. **How many blocks are there in all?**

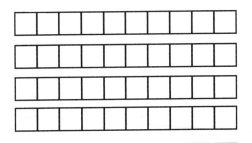

- (A) 402
- (B) 6
- (C) 42
- (D) 24

GO ON

Name _____   Date_____

12. How many blocks in all?

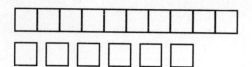

- (F) 70
- (G) 16
- (H) 7
- (J) 106

13. Which number is fifty-seven?

- (A) 507
- (B) 157
- (C) 57
- (D) 12

14. Which symbol will make this number sentence true?

34 ◯ 38

- (F) >
- (G) =
- (H) <

15. Which symbol will make this number sentence true?

12 ◯ 11

- (A) >
- (B) <
- (C) =

STOP

MATH PRACTICE TEST

Part 2: Computation

Directions: Solve these addition and subtraction problems. Choose the best answer for the question. If none of the answer choices is correct, choose "None of these." Be sure to pay attention to the sign. Practice together with examples A and B. Do the same for 1–18.

Examples

A.
$$6$$
$$\underline{+\ 4}$$
- (A) 64
- (B) 10
- (C) 2
- (D) None of these

B. $4 - 1 =$
- (F) 14
- (G) 5
- (H) 3
- (J) None of these

---

1. $4 + 9 = \square$
- (A) 13
- (B) 49
- (C) 5
- (D) None of these

2. $8 - 2 = \square$
- (F) 12
- (G) 10
- (H) 6
- (J) None of these

3. $3 + 8 = \square$
- (A) 11
- (B) 5
- (C) 38
- (D) None of these

4.
$$3$$
$$\underline{+\ 3}$$
- (F) 6
- (G) 0
- (H) 33
- (J) None of these

5.
$$12$$
$$\underline{+\ 5}$$
- (A) 124
- (B) 17
- (C) 7
- (D) None of these

6.
$$10$$
$$\underline{-\ 5}$$
- (F) 15
- (G) 105
- (H) 60
- (J) None of these

GO ON

Name _____   Date _____

7.
$$\begin{array}{r} 7 \\ -\ 7 \\ \hline \end{array}$$

- (A) 14
- (B) 7
- (C) 0
- (D) None of these

8.
$$\begin{array}{r} 25 \\ +\ 1 \\ \hline \end{array}$$

- (F) 26
- (G) 251
- (H) 35
- (J) None of these

9. $1 + 8 = \square$

- (A) 180
- (B) 90
- (C) 18
- (D) None of these

10. $15 - 2 = \square$

- (F) 13
- (G) 17
- (H) 132
- (J) None of these

11.
$$\begin{array}{r} 7 \\ -\ 3 \\ \hline \end{array}$$

- (A) 4
- (B) 37
- (C) 10
- (D) None of these

12.
$$\begin{array}{r} 19 \\ +\ 0 \\ \hline \end{array}$$

- (F) 109
- (G) 190
- (H) 0
- (J) None of these

1-57768-721-3 *Spectrum Test Practice 1*

MATH PRACTICE TEST
Part 2: Computation (cont.)

13. $1 + 2 + 1 = \square$

(A) 4

(B) 12

(C) 0

(D) None of these

16. $5 + 2 + 2 = \square$

(F) 5

(G) 9

(H) 54

(J) None of these

14.
$$\begin{array}{r} 9 \\ + \ 9 \\ \hline \end{array}$$

(F) 90

(G) 18

(H) 81

(J) None of these

17.
$$\begin{array}{r} 17 \\ - \ 7 \\ \hline \end{array}$$

(A) 10

(B) 87

(C) 114

(D) None of these

15. $17 + 2 = \square$

(A) 37

(B) 1,222

(C) 19

(D) None of these

18. $0 + 10 = \square$

(F) 0

(G) 100

(H) 10

(J) None of these

STOP

1-57768-721-3 *Spectrum Test Practice 1*

MATH PRACTICE TEST

● Part 3: Applications

Directions: Listen to your teacher read the questions. Look at the answer choices. Choose the best answer for the question. Practice with example A. Do the same for numbers 1–16.

Example

A. Bobbie read 2 books. Howie read 3 books. How many did they read all together?

 Ⓐ

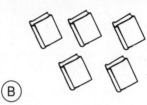 Ⓑ

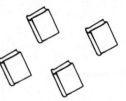 Ⓒ

---

1. The phone rang 3 times in the morning. It rang 6 times last night. How many times did it ring?

Ⓐ $3 + 3 = 6$

Ⓑ $3 + 6 = 9$

Ⓒ $6 - 3 = 3$

2. I raked 4 bags of leaves. Tyler raked 4 bags. Jess raked 2 bags. How many bags did we end up having?

Ⓕ $4 + 4 + 2 = 6$

Ⓖ $4 + 4 + 2 = 10$

Ⓗ $4 - 4 + 2 = 2$

3. Count each group of coins. Which group is worth the most?

Ⓐ

Ⓑ

Ⓒ

4. Molly had 43¢. She lost 10¢. How much did she have left?

Ⓕ 7¢

Ⓖ 33¢

Ⓗ 42¢

GO ON

1-57768-721-3 *Spectrum Test Practice 1*

5. Look at the digital clock. Which round clock shows the same time?

(A)

(B)

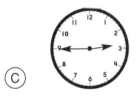

(C)

6. Amy left at 7:00. Which clock shows the time she left?

(F)

(G)

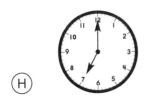

(H)

7. Look at the ruler. Look at the lines. How long is the shortest line?

(A) 2 inches

(B) 4 inches

(C) 6 inches

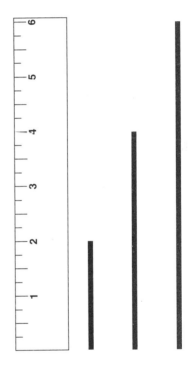

8. How many months are in one year?

(F) 11

(G) 6

(H) 12

GO ON

MATH PRACTICE TEST
Part 3: Applications (cont.)

9. **How many sides does a rectangle have?**

   (A) 3

   (B) 5

   (C) 4

10. **Which shape is not the same as the one on the left?**

  (F)

  (G)

  (H)

11. **Look at the shapes. Which shape can be folded on the dotted line so that the two sides match perfectly?**

   (A)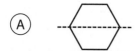

   (B)

   (C)

12. **What is the name of this shape?**

   (F) circle

   (G) oval

   (H) hexagon

GO ON

   1-57768-721-3 *Spectrum Test Practice 1*

MATH PRACTICE TEST
Part 3: Applications (cont.)

Exercise

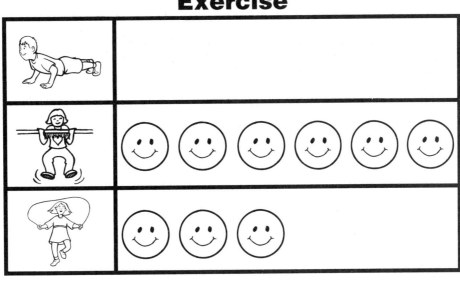

☺ = 1 Student

Look at the chart. It shows which exercises are the most liked by the class. Use it to answer 13–16.

13. How many students liked push-ups?

   Ⓐ 0

   Ⓑ 5

   Ⓒ 3

14. Which exercise was the most liked?

   Ⓕ pull-ups

   Ⓖ jump rope

   Ⓗ push-ups

15. How many students liked either push-ups and pull-ups? Choose the number sentence that solves this problem.

   Ⓐ 3 + 6 = 9

   Ⓑ 6 + 0 = 6

   Ⓒ 0 + 5 = 5

16. How many more students liked pull-ups than jumping rope?

   Ⓕ 6 − 5 = 1

   Ⓖ 6 − 3 = 3

   Ⓗ 6 + 5 = 11

STOP

● **Lesson 1: Science**

Directions: Listen to your teacher read the story and the question. Listen to each answer choice. Choose the best answer for the question. Practice with example A.

Example

Pollution Control

We need our earth. We must take care of it. One way is to keep the earth clean. When air, water, or land are dirty, they are called polluted. Smoke gets in the air. Trash pollutes the land. Chemicals get in the water.

A. **How can we care for the earth?**

Ⓐ keep it clean
Ⓑ put smoke in the air
Ⓒ throw trash out the window

 Clue Listen to the whole story before answering the question.

● **Practice**

The Season of Fall

Fall is the season after summer. Many things happen in the fall. It can be cool in the fall. The days are shorter. It is dark longer.

Plants begin to change. Some leaves change color.

Some plants stop growing. Other plants die. The fruit from plants gets ripe. People pick the fruit.

Animals change too. Some find safe places to sleep all winter. Other animals change color. Some move to warmer places until spring comes back.

1. **When is fall?**

Ⓐ after summer
Ⓑ after winter
Ⓒ before spring

2. **What happens to some leaves?**

Ⓕ they grow bigger
Ⓖ they change color
Ⓗ some become flowers

3. **Why do people pick fruit in the fall?**

Ⓐ It is ripe.
Ⓑ It is rotten.
Ⓒ The fruit is sour.

4. **Why do some animals move to a warmer place?**

Ⓕ to sleep
Ⓖ to hide from monkeys
Ⓗ to stay warm

═══ SOCIAL STUDIES ═══

◗ Lesson 1: Social Studies

Directions: Listen to your teacher read the story and the question. Listen to each answer choice. Choose the best answer for the question. Practice with example A.

Example

Food Facts

Food is important. It helps keep us alive. People eat many different things. Some like meat. They might eat beef, chicken, or pork. Some people eat only vegetables. They are called vegetarians. They like carrots, potatoes, and broccoli. Many people eat grains and fruits.

A. What might a vegetarian eat?
- (A) chicken
- (B) beef
- (C) carrots

 Clue **Listen to all of the answer choices before making your decision.**

◗ Practice

Three Friends

My name is Jamal. I live in a yellow house. I have two brothers. My mom stays at home with us. Daddy is a truck driver. We all like to swim. Every summer we all go to the beach.

My name is Juan. I was born in Mexico. I live with my grandparents in a big trailer. We have three cats and a bird. I love school. Science is my best subject. I love learning about animals.

I am Connie. I live with my mother. We have a nice apartment. She works very hard at a bakery. She makes pretty cakes. Sometimes we go to see movies together. I have fun visiting my dad on weekends.

1. How many brothers does Jamal have?
- (A) three
- (B) none
- (C) two

2. Who was born in Mexico?
- (F) Connie
- (G) Juan
- (H) Jamal

3. Why might Connie visit her dad on weekends?
- (A) He does not live with her.
- (B) She goes to the movies.
- (C) She lives with her grandparents.

 STOP

ANSWER SHEET

STUDENT'S NAME

LAST											FIRST						MI
A	A	A	A	A	A	A	A	A	A	A	A	A	A	A	A	A	A
B	B	B	B	B	B	B	B	B	B	B	B	B	B	B	B	B	B
C	C	C	C	C	C	C	C	C	C	C	C	C	C	C	C	C	C
D	D	D	D	D	D	D	D	D	D	D	D	D	D	D	D	D	D
E	E	E	E	E	E	E	E	E	E	E	E	E	E	E	E	E	E
F	F	F	F	F	F	F	F	F	F	F	F	F	F	F	F	F	F
G	G	G	G	G	G	G	G	G	G	G	G	G	G	G	G	G	G
H	H	H	H	H	H	H	H	H	H	H	H	H	H	H	H	H	H
I	I	I	I	I	I	I	I	I	I	I	I	I	I	I	I	I	I
J	J	J	J	J	J	J	J	J	J	J	J	J	J	J	J	J	J
K	K	K	K	K	K	K	K	K	K	K	K	K	K	K	K	K	K
L	L	L	L	L	L	L	L	L	L	L	L	L	L	L	L	L	L
M	M	M	M	M	M	M	M	M	M	M	M	M	M	M	M	M	M
N	N	N	N	N	N	N	N	N	N	N	N	N	N	N	N	N	N
O	O	O	O	O	O	O	O	O	O	O	O	O	O	O	O	O	O
P	P	P	P	P	P	P	P	P	P	P	P	P	P	P	P	P	P
Q	Q	Q	Q	Q	Q	Q	Q	Q	Q	Q	Q	Q	Q	Q	Q	Q	Q
R	R	R	R	R	R	R	R	R	R	R	R	R	R	R	R	R	R
S	S	S	S	S	S	S	S	S	S	S	S	S	S	S	S	S	S
T	T	T	T	T	T	T	T	T	T	T	T	T	T	T	T	T	T
U	U	U	U	U	U	U	U	U	U	U	U	U	U	U	U	U	U
V	V	V	V	V	V	V	V	V	V	V	V	V	V	V	V	V	V
W	W	W	W	W	W	W	W	W	W	W	W	W	W	W	W	W	W
X	X	X	X	X	X	X	X	X	X	X	X	X	X	X	X	X	X
Y	Y	Y	Y	Y	Y	Y	Y	Y	Y	Y	Y	Y	Y	Y	Y	Y	Y
Z	Z	Z	Z	Z	Z	Z	Z	Z	Z	Z	Z	Z	Z	Z	Z	Z	Z

SCHOOL

TEACHER

FEMALE ◯ MALE ◯

BIRTH DATE

MONTH		DAY		YEAR	
JAN ◯		0	0		0
FEB ◯		1	1		1
MAR ◯		2	2		2
APR ◯		3	3		3
MAY ◯			4		4
JUN ◯			5	5	5
JUL ◯			6	6	6
AUG ◯			7	7	7
SEP ◯			8	8	8
OCT ◯			9	9	9
NOV ◯				0	
DEC ◯					

GRADE

1 2 3 4 5

Part 1: SCIENCE

A	A B C
1	A B C
2	F G H
3	A B C
4	F G H

Part 2: SOCIAL STUDIES

A	A B C
1	A B C
2	F G H
3	A B C
4	F G H

SCIENCE AND SOCIAL STUDIES PRACTICE TEST

Part 1: Science

Directions: Listen to your teacher read the story and the question. Listen to each answer choice. Choose the best answer for the question. Practice with example A.

Example

Mammals

Mammals are a type of animals. Most mammals have hair or fur. They all were made to move. They move by walking, running, swimming, or flying. Mother mammals feed their babies milk. One kind of mammal is a dog. Another is a whale. Humans are mammals too!

A. **What do mother mammals feed their babies?**

Ⓐ carrots

Ⓑ milk

Ⓒ hot dogs

Liquid Matter

All things are made of some kind of matter. Liquid is a kind of matter.

Liquid has mass, that means it takes up space. It can become many shapes. Think about a puddle of water and a cup of water. Both are water and both are liquid, but they look different!

Some liquid is thick. Maple syrup is thick. Some liquid is thin and runny. Milk and water are thin and runny. Liquid can be hot, like coffee. It can be cool, like orange juice. You can see, touch, and even taste some liquids.

1. **What are all things made of?**

   Ⓐ some kind of matter

   Ⓑ wind

   Ⓒ ice

2. **What does mass mean?**

   Ⓕ is cool

   Ⓖ takes up space

   Ⓗ can freeze

3. **Name a thin and runny liquid.**

   Ⓐ syrup

   Ⓑ ice

   Ⓒ milk

4. **What is a liquid you can taste?**

   Ⓕ bark

   Ⓖ air

   Ⓗ orange juice

SCIENCE AND SOCIAL STUDIES PRACTICE TEST

● **Part 2: Social Studies**

Directions: Listen to your teacher read the story and the questions. Listen to all o the answer choices. Choose the best answer for the question. Practice with example A.

Example

Changes

We went to visit my grandmother. Daddy said it looks very different around his old home. One thing that is different is the neighborhood. There used to be woods around the houses. He would play in them. Now there are more people. There are also many new houses being built. More schools and stores are in the neighborhood too. There are even new parks!

A. What is one change in Grandmother's neighborhood?

- Ⓐ more schools
- Ⓑ more woods
- Ⓒ stormy weather

On the Map

A map is a picture that someone has drawn. It can be of the whole world. It can show a city. A map can even be of your school. The very first maps were made from dirt, sand, or clay. Now maps are on paper, computer screens, and many other things.

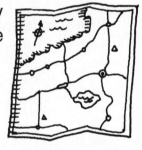

People make maps to help them remember things. Long ago, people made maps. They helped them remember where there was water or food. Now maps are made to show the way to a place. They also help people see where there are rivers, mountains, and other special places.

1. What is a map?

- Ⓐ a picture of a place
- Ⓑ a car
- Ⓒ a way to find out about dogs

2. What were the first maps made of?

- Ⓕ computers
- Ⓖ dirt, clay, and sand
- Ⓗ water

3. Why might you need a map?

- Ⓐ to find the way to a place
- Ⓑ to catch a bug
- Ⓒ for playing cards

4. Who might need a map for their job?

- Ⓕ doctor
- Ⓖ painter
- Ⓗ truck driver

STOP

Part 3: Language Expression
- A. C
- 1. B
- 2. G
- 3. C
- B. H
- 4. G
- 5. C
- 6. F
- C. B
- 7. B
- 8. F
- 9. A
- D. F
- 10. F
- 11. B

Part 4: Spelling
- A. A
- B. H
- 1. C
- 2. F
- 3. C
- 4. G
- 5. C
- 6. F
- C. C
- D. G
- 7. C
- 8. F
- 9. C
- 10. G
- 11. B
- 12. H

Part 5: Study Skills
- A. A
- 1. B
- 2. G
- 3. B
- 4. H

MATH: CONCEPTS
Lesson 1: Numeration
• Pages 104–105
- A. C
- 1. C
- 2. G
- 3. A
- 4. J
- 5. B
- 6. G
- 7. B

MATH: CONCEPTS
Lesson 2: Sequencing
• Pages 106–107
- A. A
- 1. C
- 2. H
- 3. B

- 4. G
- 5. A
- 6. G
- 7. A

MATH: CONCEPTS
Lesson 3: Number Concepts
• Pages 108–109
- A. B
- 1. B
- 2. G
- 3. C
- 4. H
- 5. C
- 6. G
- 7. B

MATH: CONCEPTS
Lesson 4: Patterns and Place Values
• Pages 110–111
- A. B
- 1. A
- 2. G
- 3. B
- 4. H
- 5. B
- 6. H

MATH: CONCEPTS
Sample Test
• Pages 112–115
- A. B
- 1. A
- 2. G
- 3. D
- 4. F
- 5. A
- 6. G
- 7. C
- 8. G
- 9. A
- 10. G
- 11. A
- 12. G
- 13. A
- 14. G
- 15. B

MATH: COMPUTATION
Lesson 5: Addition
• Pages 116–117
- A. B
- B. H
- 1. C
- 2. F
- 3. C
- 4. G
- 5. A
- 6. G
- 7. C

- 8. F
- 9. A
- 10. H

MATH: COMPUTATION
Lesson 6: Subtraction
• Pages 118–119
- A. B
- B. H
- 1. A
- 2. H
- 3. A
- 4. H
- 5. C
- 6. G
- 7. D
- 8. G
- 9. A
- 10. J

MATH: COMPUTATION
Sample Test
• Pages 120–121
- A. A
- B. J
- 1. C
- 2. F
- 3. C
- 4. F
- 5. C
- 6. H
- 7. B
- 8. J
- 9. A
- 10. H
- 11. A
- 12. H

MATH: APPLICATIONS
Lesson 7: Geometry
• Pages 122–123
- A. B
- 1. B
- 2. F
- 3. B
- 4. G
- 5. C
- 6. F
- 7. B
- 8. F

MATH: APPLICATIONS
Lesson 8: Geometry
• Pages 124–125
- A. A
- 1. B
- 2. H
- 3. C
- 4. F
- 5. C
- 6. G

7. B

MATH: APPLICATIONS
Lesson 9: Measurement
• Pages 126–127

A. C
1. B
2. F
3. B
4. G
5. C
6. H
7. A

MATH: APPLICATIONS
Lesson 10: Measurement
• Pages 128–129

A. C
1. C
2. H
3. B
4. G
5. C
6. G
7. A
8. H

MATH: APPLICATIONS
Lesson 11: Problem Solving
• Pages 130–131

A. B
1. C
2. G
3. B
4. F
5. C
6. H
7. B

MATH: APPLICATIONS
Lesson 12: Problem Solving
• Pages 132–133

A. A
B. H
1. B
2. G
3. B
4. F
5. B
6. G
7. A
8. F

MATH: APPLICATIONS
Sample Test
• Pages 134–137

A. A
1. A
2. H
3. B
4. G
5. B

6. G
7. C
8. G
9. C
10. G
11. C
12. G
13. B
14. F
15. B
16. G

MATH PRACTICE TEST
• Pages 139–149
Part 1: Concepts

A. B
1. B
2. F
3. C
4. H
5. B
6. H
7. C
8. H
9. C
10. H
11. C
12. G
13. C
14. H
15. A

Part 2: Computation

A. B
B. H
1. A
2. H
3. A
4. F
5. B
6. J
7. C
8. F
9. D
10. F
11. A
12. J
13. A
14. G
15. C
16. G
17. A
18. H

Part 3: Applications

A. B
1. B
2. G
3. A
4. G

5. C
6. H
7. A
8. H
9. C
10. H
11. A
12. G
13. A
14. F
15. B
16. G

SCIENCE
Lesson 1: Science
• Page 150

A. A
1. A
2. G
3. A
4. H

SOCIAL STUDIES
Lesson 1: Social Studies
• Page 151

A. C
1. C
2. G
3. A

SCIENCE AND SOCIAL STUDIES PRACTICE TEST
• Pages 153–154
Part 1: Science

A. B
1. A
2. G
3. C
4. H

Part 2: Social Studies

A. A
1. A
2. G
3. A
4. H